The TeMoLaYoLe book

*Te*aching *mo*dern *la*nguages to *yo*ung *le*arners: teachers, curricula and materials

THE UNIVERSITY OF
WINCHESTER

The opinions expressed in this publication are not to be regarded as reflecting the policy of any government, of the Committee of Ministers or of the Secretary General of the Council of Europe.

Cover: Gross Werbeagentur, Graz
Printer: Bachernegg, Kapfenberg
Layout: C. Stenner, Graz

http://book.coe.int
Council of Europe Publishing
F-67075 Strasbourg Cedex

European Centre for Modern Languages / Council of Europe
Nikolaiplatz 4
A-8020 Graz
Austria
www.ecml.at

ISBN: 978-92-871-6297-7
© Council of Europe, 2007

TEMOLAYOLE: what is involved and included?

Marianne Nikolov

The acronym TEMOLAYOLE stands for the teaching of modern languages to young learners and this is what this book is about. More specifically, it focuses on teachers of modern languages teaching children in primary schools, on curricula and syllabi, as well as on teaching materials and methodology. The chapters in this volume are the edited versions of ten selected papers presented at the TeMoLaYoLe: Research into Teaching Modern Languages to Young Learners Conference, which took place between 1 and 3 February 2007 (for a full programme please visit www.pte.hu/temolayole). The event was jointly organised by the European Centre for Modern Languages (ECML), Graz, and the University of Pécs, Hungary. It was also one of the highlights and a major event of the TEMOLAYOLE project hosted and sponsored by the ECML. The editors of this publication are members of the TEMOLAYOLE team.

The aim of this volume is to provide insights into what we consider good practice, innovation and quality research in recent language pedagogy. The ten papers look into issues in both pre- and in-service teacher education, innovative curriculum and syllabus design in tertiary education and lower primary schools, and how new ideas can be implemented at national and classroom levels.

The first six papers in the edited volume focus on teacher education curricula and teachers' development in pre-service and in-service programmes, whereas the last four papers look into curricula, teaching materials and projects in primary schools.

The first chapter is a comparative analysis of two special programmes that aim to develop teachers of young learners in Croatia and Slovenia. Both countries can boast of a tradition of early modern foreign language education and teacher development courses aiming to boost teachers' competencies in the domain of young learners. Marija Andraka and Mateja Dagarin evaluate their curricula and provide valuable information on the content and delivery of their programmes. They demonstrate how new areas of expertise can be integrated into traditional curricula.

In the second chapter, Gun Lundberg describes and analyses a three-year action research project in Swedish in-service teacher education for language teachers of young learners. She draws on her experience with 160 teachers participating in a programme challenging common routines, as teachers applied a research-based, age-appropriate methodology based on their learners' needs.

The third paper, written by Małgorzata Szulc-Kurpaska, gives an account of a project involving pre-service trainees at a college in Poland. Young trainees faced many problems when they were placed in kindergartens and tried to involve 5- and 6-year-old children in nicely designed activities in English. The paper shows how would-be teachers managed young children, overcame difficulties and benefited from this new opportunity.

The next chapter also focuses on teachers, but from a different angle. Mariola Bogucka discusses how Polish teachers of young language learners make sense of their profession, how they perceive their role and what career options they see for themselves in the long run. Interestingly, teachers in her project emphasise their successes with young language learners and do not long for more social recognition.

Two chapters explore how stories can be integrated into the curriculum. In one of them, Marina Mattheoudakis, Katerina Dvorakova and Katalin Láng give an account of their experimental project implemented in three countries: Greece, the Czech Republic and Hungary. They applied a module on story-based input in the methodology syllabus for the teaching of foreign languages to young learners. The paper discusses not only how pre-service teachers managed tasks related to stories, but also their reflections on their performances.

The use of narrative in early programmes is discussed by Réka Lugossy as well, but she provides insights into two perspectives: how teachers and their young learners benefited from using authentic picture books. Her explorations point in new directions, as she examines how different books involve boys more than traditional teaching materials, and in what ways lending children books and allowing them to take them home contributes to their literacy development.

Curriculum and continuity – key areas in early language programmes – are explored in a systematic way in Chapter 7 by Charis-Olga Papadopoulou. Her paper discusses serious overlaps, discrepancies and methodological problems in relation to teaching German to young learners. The strength of the study is that it shows what changes are necessary to ensure continuity and smooth transition across school types.

A particular content area in the early modern foreign language curriculum is highlighted in Gloria Vickov's paper as she analyses how Croatian children's own culture and identity are present in, or rather absent from, young learners' teaching materials. As she points out in Chapter 8, items present in the target language culture are represented and emphasised in coursebooks, but pupils hardly ever learn about their own culture. She argues for integration of children's cultural background and heritage into the early modern foreign language syllabus.

Chapter 9 triangulates young learners' views with those of their teachers and pre-service university students on the issue of integrating phonetics and phonology into the curriculum. Zeljka Zanchi argues that using phonetic transcription may not only allow learners to use dictionaries and become autonomous learners, but is also something children in primary schools, their teachers and university students agree with.

The last chapter in the volume discusses a very different avenue: Luisa Pellicer, in the only chapter written in French, gives a lively account of how her students benefited from the implementation of a cross-border project. As her paper illustrates, classroom teachers can motivate their learners extremely successfully, while their own reward is also ensured by seeing how their pupils manage in a new foreign language context.

As readers will see, a number of languages are involved in the papers. Besides English, French and German as target languages, the first language of the teachers and their young language learners include Croatian, Czech, Greek, Hungarian, Polish, Slovenian, Spanish and Swedish.

Acknowledgements

The editors would like to thank all contributors for their hard work and patience. We are grateful for the support the ECML has given us.

Contents

Chapter 1
Evaluation of teacher training programmes for primary teachers of English – A comparative study

Mateja Dagarin and Marija Andraka

1.   Introduction

The aim of this chapter is to give an account of the evaluation of early English language teacher training programmes at the Faculty of Education in Ljubljana and the Faculty of Teacher Education in Zagreb. It was felt that there was a need for feedback on the quality of teacher training programmes in order to analyse the current state of teacher training and to introduce possible changes and improvements following the results obtained by the research. For this purpose a questionnaire was designed containing two groups of questions – open-ended and closed questions. The questionnaire was then distributed to a number of in-service and pre-service students at the respective faculties and to a number of teachers who graduated from these faculties and were at the time employed as teachers of English to young learners. Results have shown that everyone included in the programmes gave similar answers regarding most issues. All the examinees expressed the need for more classroom practice, more interactive work and more practical work in general, and stressed the relevance of cross-curricular activities. As a result of the questionnaire, some changes have been made in the programmes and more changes will be introduced in the near future, in line with the Bologna Process, which has been implemented in both countries.

Training FL teachers and learning languages from an early age are currently two central issues in language education across Europe. These issues have also been emphasised by the Council of Europe, whose members have put forward early language learning as a main priority in European education. At the March 2002 meeting, heads of state and government called for a sustained effort "to improve the mastery of basic skills, in particular by teaching at least two foreign languages from a very early age" (Eurydice, 2005, p. 3). The same aims were stressed in the action plan for Promoting language learning and linguistic diversity (2003), where, besides their plan for "mother tongue plus two other languages from an early age", the report discusses the need for qualified language teachers of young learners.

In line with these aims, the authors of this article have decided to investigate the quality of early language teacher education programmes in their countries, namely Croatia and Slovenia. The two programmes, which are similar in nature, are first described and compared in detail. The main part of the article focuses on the research conducted in both countries. Pre-service and in-service students, as well as primary teachers of

English who graduated from the programmes, evaluate the respective programmes and give suggestions for their improvement. In the final part of the paper, conclusions and the changes in the programmes that have followed the research are described.

2.   Description of teacher training programmes for primary teachers of English

2.1   Slovenian teacher training programme for primary teachers of English

In Slovenia a formal need for educating teachers for teaching foreign languages to children appeared quite late, namely in the early 1990s. Before that period, young learners were mostly taught by enthusiastic teachers, who were learning early foreign language methodology on the spot. At that time, children began to learn a foreign language (89% of them English) in Year 5, when they were 11 years old. In 1990, under the project Foreign languages in primary school (Čagran, 1996), English was implemented experimentally into Years 3 and 4 (children aged 9 and 10) in some schools. The project served as the basis for putting early language learning into practice. However, the need for appropriately qualified teachers soon emerged. English language teachers who graduated from the Faculty of Arts had excellent linguistic skills, but their methodological skills varied, due to the fact that they had no special training in teaching children. Therefore, it was agreed by different stakeholders that the most appropriate option for teaching foreign languages to young learners was the classroom teacher with special training in teaching a foreign language. A new programme for training pre- and in-service classroom teachers to teach English was launched at the Faculty of Education in 1998. It was carried out in two modes until 2002:

1.   as an additional elective intended for full-time students of the four-year university Classroom education programme;

2.   as a two-year in-service teacher training programme for classroom teachers (primary school teachers) who had already finished the Classroom education programme.

In the year 2002, the last generation of full-time students was enrolled as a result of a new way of financing university programmes. At present, the programme is open only to practising teachers. Upon completion of the programme, teachers are awarded a certificate which qualifies them to teach a foreign language to children up to Year 6 (age 12). Teachers can teach English or Italian, depending on which language they have studied.

10

The aim of the programme is to educate classroom teachers to be linguistically and methodologically prepared to teach foreign languages to children. Classroom teachers are very often already methodologically well equipped as they attend courses on child psychology, pedagogy, didactics, etc. Therefore, the focus is on developing their language competence. The programme is divided into six courses with a total of 750 hours. Some 525 hours are intended for developing teachers' linguistic skills, 135 hours for developing their methodological knowledge and 90 hours are dedicated to literature.

The language module consists of 285 hours of practical English classes, 180 hours of grammar for teachers and 60 hours of phonetics and phonology. In practical English classes teachers work on the four language skills and vocabulary, in the grammar classes they improve their knowledge of language structures, and in phonetics and phonology they work on their pronunciation by practising in a language lab and recording their own speech in various situations.

The methodology module consists of 90 hours of methodology for teaching foreign languages to children and of 45 hours of a course teachers are especially fond of, that is non-verbal means of communication. Here, teachers learn how they can teach a foreign language through art, music, movement and puppetry.

The literature module comprises 30 hours of general literature in a foreign language and 60 hours of children's literature, where students learn how to select, adapt and apply stories, poems, rhymes and other literary texts in their teaching.

The programme is quite strenuous for in-service teachers. They have 12-15 lessons every weekend (Friday afternoons and Saturdays) and they need to work very hard at home as well. As a result, many of them have dropped out of the programme or have not finished it yet. The programme as such needs to be improved, and, most of all, it needs to become a regular pre-service national programme.

2.2   Croatian teacher training programme for primary teachers of English

In the last three decades of the 20th century a number of projects were launched in Croatia (cf. Vilke and Vrhovac, 1993; Vilke, et al., 1995; Vrhovac, 2001) with the aim of investigating the possibilities of an earlier introduction of foreign language learning in primary education. In this climate, the study of English as part of pre-service study for primary teachers was created at the then Teacher Education Academy in Zagreb (now the Faculty of Teacher Education). In designing the programme for the education of primary teachers of English, the basic criteria were the needs of modern EFL teaching, on the one hand, and the characteristics of the primary teacher who has responsibility to teach a foreign language to young learners, on the other.

A good primary teacher of English can meet the demands of the teaching process – in other words, a teacher who is creative, flexible, well informed, open to new ideas, knows the needs of his/her students, is ready to co-operate with his/her peers and his/her students, a teacher who is tolerant, and, of course, possesses a well-developed linguistic competence in the foreign language he/she teaches.

That is why the programme, which was launched in 1994, comprised three main areas: (1) language; (2) literature and culture; and (3) ELT methodology. It is important to point out that particular attention was paid not only to the content of the courses but also to the specific way of organising students' activities and obligations during the study (Narančić Kovač, Andraka and Antunac, 2002). This made it easier to adapt the whole programme to the requirements of the Bologna Process since some of the demands, such as continuous assessment and active involvement of students, were already part of this programme.

The following principles were put forward: interdisciplinarity, variety of content, reliance on results of research, co-ordination among the courses (to avoid overlaps and enable continuity), extra-curricular activities and projects, co-operation, tolerance and the right to a different opinion, a personal touch in teaching. Also, one of the aims was creating a positive learning climate (ibid.). An important factor which the designers of the programme had to keep in mind was the fact that their students were at the same time being trained to become primary teachers and attend courses on developmental psychology, school psychology, pedagogy, didactics, the philosophy of education, special needs pedagogy and others.

The programme comprised 12 courses with a total of 1 185 hours distributed over four years and was divided into the three mentioned areas in the following way: 570 hours of language, 405 hours of literature and culture, and 210 hours of ELT methodology. The main aim of the language module was to develop students' linguistic and communicative competence through a series of courses: language exercises, introduction to English grammar, phonetics and phonology, speaking and communication, modern English and academic writing.

The culture and literature section was covered by the course entitled "The Anglo-Saxon world", which raised the students' awareness about the impact of cultural context on language through topics taught at primary level, such as holidays, food, pop culture and others. The structure of the literature courses (selected passages from English literature, storytelling and singing, children's literature in English) was tailored so that they would complement each other and cover the basic theoretical terminology, the skills of teaching through storytelling and dramatisation, as well as the theoretical, historical and methodological aspects of children's literature. Finally, the ELT section was covered by the ELT methodology and English across the curriculum courses. They pursued the specific features of teaching English with particular reference to young learners and to the integration of English in other curriculum areas. Classroom practice was also part of these courses.

3.   Evaluation of the teacher training programmes

3.1   Aim of the study

Since both the Slovenian and the Croatian teacher training programmes were subject to constant scrutiny and evaluation with the purpose of improving them, one of the ways to analyse the current state of teacher education was to conduct a survey with both Croatian and Slovenian students and graduates from both universities. The results obtained from the research have been used to implement changes in the programmes and further improve them.

3.2   Participants

In Slovenia the questionnaire was sent to 85 participants (students and graduates). Some 51 students (60%) returned the questionnaire. These were 21 in-service students and 28 pre-service students. Two students did not specify the type of group. In Croatia the questionnaire was sent to 58 participants (pre-service students and graduates). Some 32 of them (55%) returned the questionnaire.

3.3   Instrument

A questionnaire consisting of eight questions of a closed type and four open questions was distributed to the students/graduates at the Faculty of Education in Ljubljana and the Faculty of Teacher Education in Zagreb. All the students had, at the time the survey was conducted, completed all the courses of their respective programmes.
In the closed questions section (see below), participants circled numbers from 1 to 5 indicating their agreement (1 meaning a low level of agreement and 5 meaning a high level of agreement). The questionnaire was administered in English.

Questions

1. The content of the programme was relevant to my needs as a teacher of English to young learners.

    1   2   3   4   5

2. Some content of the programme should be radically changed.

    1   2   3   4   5

3. Most of the content in the programme was appropriate.

    1   2   3   4   5

4. The teaching methods were appropriate.

1	2	3	4	5

5. The assessment tasks were appropriate.

1	2	3	4	5

6. The content of assessment tasks was relevant to my future work.

1	2	3	4	5

7. The timing of the programme was appropriate.

1	2	3	4	5

8. The information about the programme was appropriate.

1	2	3	4	5

In the second part participants were asked to provide answers to the following open questions:

1. What were you satisfied with (for example, content of the programme, execution of the programme, organisation, etc.)?

2. Do you think anything should be changed in the programme? If yes, suggest what.

3. Do you think the number of hours in each course was appropriate? If not, name the courses.

4. Write any other suggestions for improvement.

3.4 Results and discussion

3.4.1 Answers to closed questions

The results show that, although the programmes at the two faculties were not the same, there is a high degree of agreement among participants. Students generally thought the content of the programmes was relevant to their needs and were satisfied with it. Croatian students assessed very highly the teaching methods used in the courses they attended (4.68), whereas the Slovenian students were more critical (3.63). A large number of students considered assessment tasks to be appropriate (Slovenia: 3.80, Croatia: 4.31). Few students thought radical changes should be introduced in the programmes; here again, there is a difference in favour of the Croatian programme (1.19). The mean for the timing of the programmes was 3.53 for Slovenian students. On the other hand, Croatian students viewed the time of execution more favourably.

Students at both faculties thought they were very well-informed about the respective programmes.

Table 1: Means for closed questions for Slovenia and Croatia

Questions	Means Slovenia	Means Croatia
1. The content of the programme was relevant to my needs as a teacher of English to young learners.	4.14	4.54
2. Some content of the programme should be radically changed.	3.22	2.03
3. Most of the content in the programme was appropriate.	4.02	4.81
4. The teaching methods were appropriate.	3.63	4.68
5. The assessment tasks were appropriate.	3.80	4.31
6. The content of assessment tasks was relevant to my future work.	3.45	4.34
7. The timing of the programme was appropriate.	3.53	4.13
8. The information about the programme was appropriate.	4.59	4.56

3.4.2 Answers to open questions

A qualitative approach was applied to the analysis of answers to the open questions; the answers are discussed in the sequence of the questions.

1. What were you satisfied with (for example, content of the programme, execution of the programme, organisation, etc.)?

Slovenia: students were mostly satisfied with the content (for example, children's literature, ELT methodology, practical English classes, etc.). They were satisfied with most of the university lecturers, with the module-type organisation and information about the programme, as well as the extra-curricular activities, for example, workshops by foreign lecturers.

Croatia: students were also very satisfied with the content of the courses (in most cases they emphasised the courses storytelling and singing, ELT and classroom practice, and children's literature as the most useful ones), the methods used in teaching, the organisation, the availability of the lecturers and the valuable tips which prepared them for classroom work.

2. Do you think anything should be changed in the programme? If yes, specify what.

Slovenia: students mostly wanted more practical work and less theory (for example, in phonetics and ELT methodology), they wanted more hours for these courses, they would have liked to have more speaking practice in practical English classes, they thought the schedule was too tight and the content of some courses was too detailed (for example, verbs and morphology). Furthermore, they expressed the need for more classroom practice and for exposure to practical examples of teaching (for example, how to construct tests, how to teach grammar, etc.).

Croatia: some 15 students thought nothing should be changed in the programme and made no suggestions. Some thought they needed more classroom practice, especially focusing on the differences in teaching young learners and teenagers, and on teaching grammar to young learners. Seven students specifically mentioned the need for more assessment tasks. A few of them said they would have preferred to have more language practice through grammar exercises, debates, interviews and presentations.

3. Do you think the number of hours in each course was appropriate? If not, name the courses.

Slovenia: some 27 students (53%) thought that the number was inappropriate. They would have liked to have more lessons in children's literature, ELT methodology, phonetics and puppetry. Some 24 students (47%) thought the number of hours in each course was appropriate.

Croatia: some 17 students (53%) thought the number of course hours was appropriate. Four of them would have liked to have more lessons in children's literature, whereas eight students would have preferred to have learned more about assessment. Six students said there was not enough classroom practice. Two students thought the academic writing course was too extensive.

4. Write any other suggestions for improvement.

Slovenia: the students would like more practical work, fewer lectures and more autonomous work. They considered the programme very tiring and packed, especially in-service teachers, who attended lessons after their regular teaching job.

Croatia: respondents also want fewer lectures and more workshops and active participation in the courses. It is interesting to point out that nine primary teachers who already had some teaching experience mentioned the discrepancy between the university study situation and real work regarding the teaching aids and materials they had at their disposal. These teachers were employed in small schools in small towns or villages, which leads us to the tentative conclusion that state primary schools in Croatia do not cater equally for the needs of their students.

3.4.3   A comparison of the two programmes

The small differences in the replies in favour of the Croatian programme (particularly regarding the content and appropriateness of the programme, assessment tasks and the time of execution of the programme) can be attributed to the fact that the Croatian programme is a pre-service course spread over a period of four years; the number of courses and hours in the courses was greater, and the participants were full-time students. On the other hand, the Slovenian programme is now only an in-service course, with students who have regular teaching jobs, most of whom have families and small children and, consequently, they find the programme quite demanding. They do not like the timing of the programme (that is, weekends), but it is the only possible time when they can all attend courses, since they come from different parts of Slovenia and some even from abroad. Lower evaluation of the content and appropriateness of the programme can also be ascribed to the fact that the university lecturers who teach in the programme come from two different faculties and they did not co-ordinate their work.

In Slovenia, the results of the evaluation can already be felt. After the evaluation, a meeting was held where all the mentioned points were openly discussed and some resolutions were made. The first resolution was the co-operation between different courses. It was decided that lecturers need to co-operate more and plan at least some work together. The methodological thread has to be felt in all courses – in this way, the lack of hours in the ELT methodology module could be compensated for. Grammar classes are therefore becoming more "child-oriented" with, for instance, the discussion of language structures in stories and rhymes; lessons in ELT methodology are getting more practical as well, with needs analysis preceding the lectures. In general, there is more interactive work in the majority of the courses. As far as the timing of the programme is concerned, not much could be changed, but there is hope that with launching the new programme, which is being designed at the moment, this could be improved as well.

The structure and the aims of the new programme were constructed with the help of teachers who teach foreign languages to children and consultants from Slovenia and abroad, who observed English language lessons and who contributed with their experience, having already designed similar programmes. The evaluation of the programme described in this article, together with meetings and discussions with teachers also helped us immensely in designing the programme. Furthermore, we followed some of the Bologna suggestions and the guidelines written in the document *European profile for language teacher education – A frame of reference* (2004). The new programme will offer 20 compulsory courses and nine electives. Some of the courses have not been changed, but most of them have been modified and now focus more on teaching young learners. Some courses have been added, for example, assessment, role play and drama in a young-learner classroom, intercultural and inter-language awareness and classroom language, to name just a few. The programme consists of 1 140 hours which add up to 103 ECTS points, together with three electives and the teaching practice, which has also been extended to between 80 and 90 hours altogether during the four years of study. The programme has not been implemented yet, but we hope it will be in two years' time.

In Croatia, the results of the questionnaire also contributed to some changes in the programme. The timing of the survey coincided with the changes introduced at all Croatian universities with the implementation of the Bologna Process in 2005. A new programme was designed and is now in the second year of its implementation. It is similar to and aligned on foreign language teacher education programmes in Europe regarding its theoretical and methodological content, as well as in relation to the emphasis placed on the interdisciplinary approach, intercultural attitudes, new technologies, on developing strategies of learner autonomy and self-assessment, etc. (Programme of Undergraduate and Graduate Study of Primary Education (A Major) in Combination with the Study of the English Language (B Major), 2005.)

The programme also serves an essential purpose in respect of the needs of the Croatian education system, especially as foreign language learning has become compulsory from Year 1 of primary school (since the school year 2003/04). In addition, students are encouraged to learn at least two foreign languages in the lower secondary grades. This means that educational authorities have finally recognised and acknowledged the need for all students to attain an acceptable communicative level in the English language during their education as well as the necessity to provide well-educated and competent teachers of English for all students from the very beginning of their compulsory education. The new programme of study incorporates 27 compulsory courses and between 3 and 8 electives. The compulsory programme comprises 1, 290 teaching hours plus teaching practice in English, and 93 ECTS points. Each elective course comprises an additional 30 teaching hours and 2 ECTS points (ibid.).

One of the immediate consequences of the survey results was the introduction of a new one-semester course dedicated exclusively to evaluation and assessment. Moreover, the number of hours in the ELT methodology module has been increased to 315, with teaching practice covering one third of it (105 hours), and five weeks of additional practice have been introduced over a period of five semesters. Additionally, in some of the courses, students are required to keep a portfolio, in order to become acquainted with the practice of portfolio assessment and to implement it later in their teaching practice with greater ease.

4. Conclusions

The survey has shown which areas in the programmes are strong and which could be improved. A similar survey could also be conducted in other countries with comparable programmes. Nevertheless, the evaluation and the suggestions probably reflect the overall wish of students across Europe, namely the need for more practical, autonomous and interactive work. Contemporary students and teachers want to take responsibility for their future careers and they do not want to enter classrooms without extensive previous practice in teaching. Furthermore, they would like to be competent in the language that they teach. Interestingly, their aims are in accordance with those of the Council of Europe. By following these guidelines and by implementing them in the reform, European programmes for educating primary school teachers destined to teach languages to young learners could produce qualified teachers, who are linguistically and methodologically well equipped. This is the key to young learners having a successful and pleasant start to learning foreign languages.

Acknowledgements: the authors would like to thank their colleagues and students for their co-operation in the survey.

References

Commission of the European Communities (2003), "Communication from the Commission to the Council, the European Parliament, the Economic and Social Committee and the Committee of the Regions. Promoting language learning and linguistic diversity: An action plan 2004-2006", Brussels, European Commission (http://ec.europa.eu/comm/education/doc/official/keydoc/actlang/act_lang_en.pdf).

Čagran, B. (1996), *Evalvacija projekta Tuji jeziki na razredni stopnji* (Project evaluation: foreign languages in lower primary school), Ljubljana, Zavod Republike Slovenije za šolstvo.

Eurydice (2005), *Key data on teaching languages at school in Europe*, Brussels, European Commission.

Fidler, S. (2002), *Evalvacijsko poročilo Študijskega programa za izpopolnjevanje učiteljic in učiteljev razrednega pouka za poučevanje angleškega jezika v drugem obdobju osnovne šole* (Evaluation report of the study programme educating classroom teachers to teach English to young learners), Ljubljana, Pedagoška fakulteta.

Kelly, M., Grenfell, M., Alan, R., Kriza., C. and McEvoy, M. (2004), "European profile for language teacher education – A frame of reference", Southampton, UK, University of Southampton. Retrieved on 22 January 2007 from http://ec.europa.eu/education/policies/lang/doc/profile_en.pdf.

Narančić Kovač, S., Andraka, M. and Antunac, M. (2002), "Izobrazba učitelja engleskog jezika – Zagrebački model" (Education of primary teachers of English – The Zagreb model), *Zbornik Učiteljske akademije u Zagrebu*, 4, 1 (4), 163-167.

"Programme of undergraduate and graduate study of primary education (A major) in combination with the study of the English language (B major)", unpublished document (2005), Zagreb, Faculty of Teacher Education.

Vilke, M. and Vrhovac, Y. (eds.) (1993), *Children and foreign languages*, Zagreb, University of Zagreb.

Vilke, M., Vrhovac, Y., Kruhan, M., Sironić-Bonefačić, N. and Skender, I. (eds.) (1995), *Children and foreign languages*, Zagreb, University of Zagreb.

Vrhovac, Y. (ed.) (2001), *Children and foreign languages*, Zagreb, University of Zagreb.

About the authors

Mateja Dagarin, Ph.D., is an assistant professor at the Faculty of Education in Ljubljana, Slovenia, where she teaches courses in TEFL methodology specialising in teaching young learners. Her interests include developing young learners' oral communicative skills, language and intercultural awareness, and assessing young learners.

Marija Andraka is a Senior Lecturer at the Faculty of Teacher Education in Zagreb, Croatia, where she teaches courses in TEFL methodology specialising in teaching young learners. Her research involves curriculum development, topic-based teaching and developing intercultural competence.

Chapter 2
Developing teachers of young learners: in-service for educational change and improvement

Gun Lundberg

1. Introduction

This paper presents a three-year action research project within in-service education for language teachers of young learners. The aims of the project were to challenge traditions and school codes, reduce the gap between visions and praxis and improve teaching and learning in young learners' language classrooms. Teaching languages to young learners is challenging, difficult and demanding. Action research can be helpful for teachers, as it allows them to systematically examine their practice and its effect on student performance, to reveal much of what is taken for granted about teaching and learning of languages and to provide opportunities for self-discovery to improve one's own practice. In this action research project, I drew on my experience with 160 teachers participating in an in-service programme of 15 credit points (European Credit Transfer System – ECTS) at Umeå University, between 2004 and 2006. The teachers have challenged common routines and improved teaching and learning in their classrooms using a research-based, age-appropriate and individualised methodology.

2. Background to teaching languages to young learners in Sweden

Sweden has for many years suffered from a shortage of teachers appropriately trained to teach languages to young learners. In 1987 the Swedish National Agency for Higher Education decided that English should no longer be a compulsory subject within primary teacher training, instead it was offered as an optional subject within the primary teacher training courses. This resulted in English competing with other optional elements such as PE, art, music, citizenship, environmental education, ICT and so forth. This policy decision had dire consequences which resulted in only a 30% uptake for the English language option.

The general view in Sweden and beyond seems to be that all young people have a sufficient knowledge of English after finishing upper secondary education and having travelled around for a bit, diving at the Great Barrier Reef, backpacking in Thailand or maybe working in a coffee shop in London. It is an irrefutable fact that many higher education students in Sweden are very proficient in English but this does not mean that they will be competent or indeed confident enough to plan and deliver English lessons to primary-aged pupils.

Although consensus has been achieved in Europe and beyond relating to the advantages of teaching modern languages at an early age (Holmstrand, 1983; SOU, 1992, p. 22; Council of Europe, 1997; Svartvik, 1999; Ladberg, 2003), there are significant variations between regions and schools concerning the introduction of English in primary school and the implementation in actual classroom practice is still undeveloped in many schools in Sweden (Skolverket, 2005a and b). The national syllabus for English and the goals to be attained by the end of Year 5 in school (11 year olds) are very wide (Skolverket, 2001).

These wide goals can appear very attractive to a qualified teacher, educated in appropriate methodology and having access to plenty of authentic teaching material, but for an unqualified teacher these national goals are not easily transferred into practice. This is probably the main reason why the textbooks and workbooks are regarded as the most appropriate pedagogy by insecure non-specialist teachers. They seem to regard this method as a best-fit approach.

2.1   In-service for teachers of English to young learners

This contextual background was the starting point for the design of a course at Umeå University. The aim was to design an in-service course for primary teachers who are unqualified to teach English to young learners but who are obliged to do so. The unequal treatment of English as a subject in the early school years and the shortage of teachers appropriately trained to teach it to young learners raise demands on an effective in-service education with a built-in capacity for challenging traditions and the development of sustainable change and improvement towards a more communicative approach of teaching and learning in the language classroom. The earlier attempts with in-service days, weekend courses and evening classes have not been satisfactory. The limitations of so-called one shot workshops for developing new teaching strategies are obvious and well documented. Teachers would use parts of the in-service material as a "tossed salad" approach for a couple of lessons and then return to the safety of their textbooks and study kit.

The bespoke in-service opportunity was designed as a part-time, distance course of 15 ECTS points, stretching over a period of twenty weeks, the model being for teachers to divide their delivery and study time on a 50-50 basis, a perfect blend of theory and practice and a more long-term opportunity for sustainability of change. The aims were to emphasise research-based teaching and strive for a goal of better application into practise of the centralised syllabus based on the CEFR and the communicative approach to teaching and learning of languages. A further aim was to develop more confidence and autonomy in the teachers through building on sufficient competence in the target language and in age-appropriate methodology, for them to be able to realise the communicative young learners' language classroom.

An action research module was built into the course, as it is a well-known understanding that action research has a capacity to improve educational practice, promote professional development and enhance classroom performance. Action research is also understood to have a potential for long-term change and commitment through encouraging professionals to reflect critically on their often taken-for-granted practices where uncontested beliefs and values are held by staff members (Elliott, 1991, 1993, 1998, 2006; Rönnerman, 1998, 2000, 2004; Somekh, 2006). Ultimately, action research acts as a catalyst for empowerment as it is the teachers' own questions that get put on the research agenda (Burnaford, Fischer and Hobson, 2000).

2.2   Educational action research

Teaching is increasingly complex work and it is teachers and teachers only who can improve and develop language education in schools. Teachers are in the position of being able to make use of their own educational contexts to generate ideas for change and improvement they identify as important, and with action research as a tool, they are able to develop their professional learning through systematic investigation rather than by reproduction of disconnected teaching tip-offs. Through action research, teachers will begin to understand what is really happening in their classrooms (Carr and Kemmis, 1986). Action research can be understood as a natural part of teaching as to be a teacher means to observe students and study classroom interactions and to explore a variety of effective ways of teaching (Burnaford, Fisher and Hobson, 2000).

The action research model used in this in-service programme originates from the work of Lawrence Stenhouse and John Elliott in the United Kingdom during the 1970s, designated as the Teachers-as-Researchers Movement (Elliott, 1991, 1993; Stenhouse, 1985). Stenhouse and Elliott linked classroom-based research to curriculum change and innovative learning strategies, and felt that all teaching should be based upon research and that research and curriculum development were the preserve of teachers (McKernan, 1996). The action research cycle used in this context is a modified variant from Stenhouse and Elliot: initial idea; fact finding and analysis; general plan; implementation of the first action step; monitoring of implementation and effects; revising of plan; the second action step; and evaluation (Elliott, 1991).

3.   The study

At the heart of this in-service action research project laid also the challenge for me as a teacher trainer to improve my practice as an educator, so the aim can be said to be twofold. The research questions were developed along the following lines:

- What impact can action research have on the development of language teaching in the young learners' classroom?

- How do teachers and pupils view the changed educational practice?

The teachers have been free to choose their own research questions and thus it is the teachers themselves who have conducted research in their own educational contexts. Their research questions have then been categorised into five themes which can be viewed as key areas for desired school improvement concerning early language teaching and learning:

- an early start;

- target language use;

- strategies for teaching and learning;

- motivation;

- documentation and language portfolio.

As these five key areas overlap in all of the projects, it is impossible to state percentage data for every category, but the areas of an early start and target language use can be said to outnumber the other categories by far.

The triangulation technique, which was popularised by Elliott in his action research, has been used by the teachers with a variety of methods for data collection, such as classroom observations, ongoing teacher diary, field notes, pupil diaries, interviews, surveys, digital photos, filming and evaluations of all kinds. The pupils have been actively involved in the action research process of improving the teaching and learning procedure in the language classroom through various documentation tasks, surveys, interviews, self-assessment and evaluations, and the children have shown to be effective contributors to change in the language classrooms.

The action research projects have been documented in the format of a report which has encouraged the teachers to reflect and examine the process systematically by making a meta-analysis of their research. The course participants, who came from all over Sweden but with a majority originating from the northern half of the country, have carried out their action research with commitment, enthusiasm and genuine engagement, and the amount of time they have put aside for their projects is far beyond the time that was originally anticipated.

3.1   Starting point: key areas for improvement

Significant change must start with looking at our own practice, and action research acknowledges the importance of teachers' experiences as a starting point for development. The most common benchmark based on initial teacher fact finding, the very first step of the action research project, is that many teachers are insecure and lack the confidence to teach English effectively. One of the teachers describes this as, "The English lessons are like black holes which you have to fill with something". A majority of the schools involved in this research begin English in Year 3, even if the recommendation from the National Curriculum Committee in 1991 was to begin English in Year 1 (SOU, 1992, p. 22). The average amount of time set aside for English in the timetables is thirty minutes per week in Year 3 and eighty minutes per week in Years 4 and 5. Although English is a core subject together with Swedish and mathematics, the time allowance is only a quarter compared to the other two core subjects in primary school. English is commonly seen by the participant teachers as having a rather low status compared to other school subjects.

The teaching of English is said to be traditional and based on old textbooks with the emphasis on word lists containing Swedish translations and weekly homework tests, focusing on the spelling of the words of the week. Lessons are said to be teacher-centred with frequent elements of silent work, like grammar exercises and translation tasks, carried out individually. There seems to be lack of conscious long-term planning, which causes a weakness in continuity and progression, sometimes resulting in parts of the same course being taught twice, when there is a change of teacher, usually between Years 3 and 4. The use of the target language in the classroom is very infrequent amongst teachers and pupils alike. Instructions are often delivered in Swedish and if the teacher speaks English it is most likely followed by a translation into Swedish. Students explain their reluctance to use English in class by referring to feelings of embarrassment. Teachers explain their scarcity of target language use by their lack of language proficiency and communicative skills due to having had no English at all in their teacher education. The fact that the number of teachers with adequate education for teaching English is low can be said to coincide with the poor realisation of the communicative language classroom.

Given this initial baseline, the action research projects can be said to have resulted in significant progress in terms of improvement in classroom practice. It is close to mission impossible to try to alter a school culture with traditional, uncontested teaching habits and it is certainly not fully obtainable within a twenty-week time scale. However, stones have been turned and the green shoots of change have begun to materialise, which the presentation of the following evidence will show.

3.2 Improvement in teaching and learning – A summary of outcomes

The outcomes of the action research projects have been analysed and interpreted by the teachers themselves in the light of their knowledge of their educational contexts and experience. In addition to their analysis, I have conducted an interpretation and evaluation of the action research reports, according to my research questions. The analysis of the reports from six in-service courses – one course of twenty weeks each semester, over a period of three years, 2004-06 – has resulted in a variety of outcomes relating to teaching and learning in the young learners' classrooms across Sweden.

3.3   An early start

More than 25% of the action research projects focus on an early introduction of English (preschool or Year 1) and all of these projects seem to have been successful in commencing English with children as young as 6 and 7 years of age. Teachers seem to be convinced that such young children can benefit from early language learning in the same way as older pupils do. When identical introductory courses were delivered to 6 and 9 year olds, no specific learning differences were perceived according to the teachers involved.

Many of the participating teachers have been surprised at how quickly young children have picked up English and learnt songs, rhymes, words and phrases with excellent pronunciation. Another surprising outcome according to the teachers is that Swedish children do not seem to absorb and learn as much English from TV and computer games as they say they have been led to believe by school politicians, attempting to defend educational issues like the shortage of appropriately trained English teachers for young learners and the late introduction of English in many schools. According to the findings and analyses in the course participants' reports, most of the young computer players use a Swedish translation button in the games or ask a parent for translation and then simply learn which button to use automatically. Those who say that they have learnt English words from computer games give examples like English names for characters in the games or expressions like "back to base". Young children do not always even seem to be aware of particular English words as being designated as English. A case in point is that of the McDonald's hamburger menu "happy meal" which many considered a Swedish term due to its regular usage.

Children who expressed that it is easier to understand English via computer games than in the real world explained that the speaking pace is slower than in the real world. As to films on TV, DVD and cinema, Sweden is one of the few countries where subtitles are used instead of dubbing and this has long been seen as a reason for the good English pronunciation skills among Swedish people. The results of this project show that a majority of the children seem to rely on the Swedish subtitles even if some of them state that they also listen to the spoken English, and they seem to become more or less dependent on translation instead of trying to listen to the English language and practice the strategy of guessing competence. In the action research projects where the aim has been to try and raise children's awareness of the guessing strategy and its positive effects on language learning (Rubin, 1975), there seems to be an enhancement of children's awareness of the advantages of trying to reduce their dependence on subtitles and translation in favour of focusing on listening to the target language. Films and computer games used in the school context are always monolingual and English lessons are supposed to be more or less monolingual, which in reality give an advantage to learning English within a school context with exposure to movement songs, rhymes, picture books, games, total physical response and a great variety of communicative activities. The outcomes of these action research projects underline the importance of teachers and communicative classroom activities for learning a language in the early years.

Teachers have introduced so-called "English corners" and "English resource boxes" within classrooms and started to build a collection of authentic and stimulating material for pupil use. Children have been encouraged to bring English items to school and to take a variety of resources home with them in order to show picture books, sing songs or play games in English with their families. Parents have reported back to school about sisters and brothers as young as 3 or 4 starting to use English words and sing English songs, thanks to the 6 and 7 year olds proudly sharing their new English skills.

All the reports on an early start praise songs as an excellent tool for learning languages. A 6-year-old girl explained to her teacher that she thought she both understood and talked English better when she sang. Other methodological highlights for the participating teachers have been puppets, cuddly toys, total physical response activities, picture books, and the teaching strategies of continual repetition and so-called "choir activities", speaking all at the same time instead of individually, which seems to have created a secure language learning environment for all, including the teachers.

3.4   Target language use

All action research reports could be said to deal with efforts of enhancement of teachers' and students' target language use in the classroom context in one way or the other. The action research results show that it is difficult and time consuming to transform a bilingual classroom context into a monolingual one, but continuous practice seems to give positive results. The initial problems for the teachers themselves have been to try and overcome a lack of self-esteem and methodological insecurity. Through careful lesson planning and oral practice of instructions, classroom management phrases and new vocabulary beforehand, teachers seem to have gradually improved their skills of providing comprehensible input in the target language and provided learners with a richer target language environment.

The importance of consistency is raised in many reports as it is easy to give in to students shouting, "Say it in Swedish!" or "We don't understand!" By presenting vocabulary in chunks and in context rather than as isolated words or lists and by making use of songs, rhymes, visuals, puppets, toys, hands-on activities, role play, stories and a well-balanced recycling of language, teachers report that students have begun to use the target language in a more relaxed and natural way. Children seem to forget their embarrassment of speaking English when lessons are active and fun, which a young learner explained as "It is much easier to learn English when you act in English".

By careful lesson planning and by including a variety of activities, organising different student groupings and using many types of interaction, teachers feel they have been rewarded with more active, communicative and interested students. Teachers have tried to build on confidence and self-esteem exercises, fetching ideas from identity- and group-strengthening methodology, such as value education and storyline, with seemingly good results. They have also sought to incorporate concepts from the general primary curriculum to make language lessons more relevant, familiar and holistic. An overall aim has been to create a secure teaching climate in the classroom with emphasis on positive feedback and careful error correction.

The main catalyst for the transformation into a monolingual classroom seems to have been the initiating and practising of guessing competence as a strategy for understanding, where students make use of background knowledge, familiar words, pictures, body language, etc., instead of craving immediate translation into Swedish to clarify meaning. Pupils who are encouraged to make use of the strategy of guessing show a greater willingness to take risks in the classroom according to the action research projects.

Children seem to begin using more target language when they are asked to calculate their application of target language by keeping a contribution log in their English diaries each lesson. Teachers have learnt from their projects that the more children use the target language the less embarrassed they seem to feel about it, which could be interpreted as embarrassment of speaking the language seems to coincide with the lack of opportunities to practice speaking the language. A relief for all teachers who are uncomfortable with using the target language are the findings that children automatically believe that teachers are good at English so there is really no need for staff to become overanxious about their capacity, competence and skill base to develop their pupils' learning.

3.5 Strategies for teaching and learning

According to the course participants' action research reports, the teachers appear to have become more aware of the importance of effective planning, both on a short- and long-term basis, and of the importance of goal-setting and the incorporation of learning objectives to ensure pupil progression. Time spent on planning has clearly shown to be rewarding. A frequent discussion point in the reports is the question of time in connection with language teaching and learning. Many critical teacher voices have been raised about the restricted timetables determining one or two English lessons per week, as lessons of thirty minutes or more have been found to be ineffective for young learners as communicative language learning demands a lot of energy and concentration. "I don't understand English when I am tired," explains a boy of 7 in an interview. Teachers have begun to spread the lessons out during the week as their newly developed communicative approach to teaching has shown to be more successful with frequent shorter lessons instead of a longer lesson once or twice a week. The right to design your English timetable is unfortunately only reserved for the generic class teachers while peripatetic area resource teachers of English have to stick to the restricted timetable.

In order to enhance the preference for language learning and to raise pupils' awareness of applications and benefits of language learning, the teachers have initiated discussions of why languages are learnt in school. The question "Why do we have to learn a language?" seems to have been crucial in creating extrinsic motivation for language learning in these action research projects. Pupils have been found to have a surprisingly unclear view of why and how they are learning languages in school. These awareness-raising discussions seem to have had a real impact on the development of teaching because of the teachers getting useful information about pupils' views, interests and needs. This information is said to have raised teachers' awareness of what is not going on in their classrooms that really should be going on and the need to organise their teaching in order to meet their learners' interests and needs. The awareness-raising discussions seem to have made teachers more open to new methods and materials, and have resulted in textbooks being marginalised in favour of more authentic materials, such as picture books, stories, children's magazines, newspaper headlines, pictures and articles, children's films and documentaries, and communicative activities such as total physical response activities, drama and games. Teachers also seem to have begun to encourage the development of the pupils' own language production using "My English book" and "My English diary", as opposed to the traditional replication and rote learning didactic strategies as featured in traditional learning materials. English no longer seems to be an isolated subject as teachers have started to make efforts to merge it holistically into the generic skill and competence base for early learning provision. The subject is delivered increasingly through topic and thematic approaches. Teachers' increased awareness of the need for a positive, self-esteem-raising learning atmosphere in the classroom has resulted in a more well thought out handling of corrections and feedback.

A number of action research projects have focused on an even more developed child-centred approach in language teaching by introducing small steps for learner autonomy, which have been described as having been motivation- and activity-raising for the pupils involved but slightly stressful for the teachers because of colleagues' suspicious views. Teachers also describe their projects on learner autonomy as connected with an initially heavy workload but very rewarding after a couple of months.

3.6   Motivation

The challenge of motivating pupils for language learning should not be underestimated and seems to become crucial after the initial years of English, at the age of 10 or 11. According to the action research reports, teachers seem to play the central role of creating motivation in the language classroom. A successful way of making language learning more exciting and thus motivating seems, according to this study, to be to make learners more involved and participative in the planning, realisation and evaluation of teaching and learning in the language classroom. Having been consulted on a regular basis on language learning matters, pupils have generated lots of ideas to bring English alive and they have even begun to bring in authentic language material to school. Another teaching strategy for stimulating pupils' motivation seems to have been the organising of thematic work with a compulsory, common base but with a range of built-in optional activities, meeting with different interests and learning styles, where pupils have been allowed to be more responsible for designing their own learning.

With the reduced use of coursebooks in favour of more authentic and communicative material, pupils seem to have become more actively engaged during lessons and have begun to express the view that the learning of English is fun and enjoyable and they have even requested more English lessons. There is also evidence of their returning earlier from break when English is on the timetable. When the provided language input is believed to be interesting and enjoyable, English seems to be used beyond the formal lessons in a natural way and the young learners also begin to articulate their interest and motivation for English at home. Pupils start to show increased curiosity about the language in terms of words, phrases, expressions and cultural and geographical language aspects. Pupils also seem to begin using dictionaries, maps and fact books in a voluntary and self-directed manner. A handful of the action research projects emphasise that language teachers should consider whether the commonly expressed view that "English is boring" in reality seems to coincide with a lack of self-esteem when speaking English.

The most demotivating factors for early language learning according to this study are: long lessons with a slow pace and a lack of physical activities, too much revising and too few challenges, lack of variety, uninteresting material, too much silent work on your own, inconsistency of target language use and isolated lesson units without cohesion.

3.7   Documentation and language portfolio

A variety of methods and strategies for assessment and documentation have been introduced by the teachers participating in the action research project. The overall aim has been to visualise pupils' language learning and achievement in order to make pupils more aware of what they are learning in language lessons and how they are progressing. By practising individual target-setting, both for teachers and pupils, with the starting point in the national curriculum guidelines and goals to attain, pupils seem to have become more aware of what they are learning in language lessons and why they are doing certain activities. When teachers have begun to present the aims to pupils at the beginning of each lesson, alternately on a weekly or thematic period base, and constantly refer back to the aims, pupils seem to respond well and work more actively. Progression awareness seems to coincide with enhancement of motivation according to the reports, for both teachers and learners alike, which is underlined by statements like "I had no idea I was so good at English, it made me feel so happy!" (Girl, aged 9, after having evaluated documentation of a six-week learning period) and "My pupils' progression has made me much more interested in my job". Language education seems to need more evidence that teaching and learning has been successful.

Many of the projects on documentation have focused on digital portfolio and especially on documentation of children's development of oral skills, with the aim of improving their self-esteem for speaking English. Children have shown to be enthused by the recording of oral skills such as their singing, rhyming and acting, and have commented that they would like to listen to recordings of their spoken English over and over again. Teachers comment that they have learnt a lot by listening to recordings of lessons, both concerning their own English skills and the amount of teacher talk and individual children's participation in the oral activities. Some children can be heard to repeat words quietly to themselves throughout the lessons, hiding under the sound barrier from the class. A successful way of learning more about your learners, according to the action research reports, is to conduct recorded interviews with them which is easily done in the MP3 format. Documentation of oral skills helps to change focus from the traditional grammar and spelling tradition to the importance of communicative skills.

Parts of the Swedish version of the European Language Portfolio (ELP), certified in 2004, have been tried out successfully in a number of action research projects, but none of the projects have adopted the ELP on a full-scale basis while many teachers express their wish to continue the ELP work and extend it step by step. Meanwhile, students have placed their work products in their general showcase portfolios, having been encouraged to produce their own stories, plays, flashcards and so forth, and their eagerness to take pride in their achievements is reflected by the high status that the portfolios hold for them.

Documentation using digital camera and film has been frequently used by participating teachers. By creating PowerPoint presentations of the language classroom activities, teachers have been able to present their teaching ideas for parents and thus managed to make them more positive towards new methods and approaches. The PowerPoint presentations have also proved useful when revising with the children and helping them to remember all the good work they have done.

4.   Closing remarks

The most significant finding for us all in the entire action research project was the realisation of how difficult it is to bring about any change in methodology within a school culture which has strongly embedded teaching traditions. When the culture, processes and practice are so firmly rooted, then change is resisted. However, this project has shown that action research can be a useful tool for empowering language teachers and improving teaching and learning in young learners' classrooms. Maybe action research, with its cyclical characteristic with no finishing point, has a better chance of dealing with resistance in the field of education and in-service training than other models. Teachers reported that the action research model felt like a powerful form of professional development because it grew out of their own specific contexts and they were in control of the process by their planning, action and reflection.

Action research clearly seems to involve teachers more actively than traditional in-service methodology and course content, and a hypothesis that springs to mind while analysing this project is that the lack of change in language classrooms could be due to a lack of personal involvement in the target language and language education. Teachers are responsible for developing a learning environment and they are stimulators of the learning process. In fact, teachers have nearly all the power over their teaching and are thus key figures in initiating change and improvement. There are numerous examples of good practice in young learners' classrooms all over Sweden, but there are pedagogical issues not being addressed that really should be as a matter of urgency. Effective learning strategies must be embedded throughout our primary schools and qualitative teacher training, both pre-service and in-service, lies at the core of this vision but no lectures or books can replace your own analysis of the effectiveness of your own teaching and learning styles.

I would like to give voice to two of the participating teachers by sharing some of their reflections: "Suddenly it dawns on me that my learning journey will never be completed during my professional life." "I sincerely believe that we as teachers should question established practices relating to the teaching of English."

References

Burnaford, G., Fischer, J. and Hobson, D. (eds.) (2000), *Teachers doing research. The power of action through inquiry* (2nd edn), New Jersey, LEA.

Carr, W. and Kemmis, S. (1986), *Becoming critical. Education, knowledge and action research*, London, Falmer Press.

Council of Europe (1997), *Foreign language learning in primary schools*, Strasbourg, Council of Europe Publishing.

Elliott, J. (1991), *Action research for educational change*, Milton Keynes, Open University Press.

Elliott, J. (1993), *Reconstructing teacher education*, London, Falmer Press.

Elliott, J. (1998), *The curriculum experiment. Meeting the challenge of social change*, Buckingham, Open University Press.

Elliott, J. (2006), *Reflecting where the action is. The selected works of John Elliott*, London, Routledge.

Holmstrand, L. (1983), *Engelska på lågstadiet* (English in Primary school), Skolöverstyrelsen, Utbildningsforskning, FoU rapport 45, Stockholm, Liber.

Ladberg, G. (2003), *Barn med flera språk* (Children with several languages), Stockholm, Liber.

McKernan, J. (1996), *Curriculum action research* (2nd edn), London, RoutledgeFalmer.

Rubin, J. (1975), "What the 'good language learner' can teach us", *TESOL Quarterly*, 9, 43.

Rönnerman, K. (1998), *Utvecklingsarbete – En grund för lärares lärande* (Developmental work – A base for teachers' learning), Lund, Studentlitteratur.

Rönnerman, K. (2000), *Att växa som pedagog. Utvärdering av ett aktionsforskningsprojekt i förskolan* (To grow as an educationalist. Evaluation of an action research project in pre-school), Göteborg, Göteborgs universitet: IPD-rapporter No. 2000: 23.

Rönnerman, K. (ed.), (2004), *Aktionsforskning i praktiken – Erfarenheter och reflektioner* (Action research in practice – Experiences and reflections), Lund, Studentlitteratur.

Skolverket (2001), *Språk. Grundskola och gymnasieskola. Kursplaner; betygskriterier och kommentarer* (Languages. Syllabuses, grading criteria and comments), Gy 2000: 18, Stockholm, Skolverket och Fritzes.

Skolverket (2005a), *Engelska. Nationella utvärderingen av grundskolan 2003* (English. National evaluation of the compulsory school in 2003), Ämnesrapport till rapport 251, Stockholm, Fritzes.

Skolverket (2005b), *Grundskolans ämnen i ljuset av Nationella utvärderingen 2003* (The subjects of the comprehensive school in the light of the national evaluation 2003), Stockholm, Fritzes.

Somekh, B. (2006), *Action research – A methodology for change and development*, Berkshire, Open University Press.

SOU (1992), *Skola för bildning* (School for education. Policy document), 1991 års läroplanskommitté, Stockholm, Liber.

Stenhouse, L. (1985), "Research as a basis for teaching", in Ruddock, J. and Hopkins, D. (eds.), *Readings from the work of Lawrence Stenhouse*, Oxford, Heinemann Educational Books, 113-128.

Svartvik, J. (1999), *Engelska – Öspråk, världsspråk, trendspråk* (English – Island language, world language and trend language), Falun, Norstedts ordbok.

About the author

Gun Lundberg is a lecturer in the Faculty of Teacher Education at Umeå University, Sweden, where she teaches pre-service and in-service courses concerning teaching and learning of language across the curriculum, English for primary years and sustainable development. She is an international co-ordinator working with exchange programmes for teacher students in New Zealand and Australia.

Chapter 3
Teaching and researching very young learners: "They are unpredictable"

Małgorzata Szulc-Kurpaska

1.   Introduction

This chapter gives an account of a special project involving pre-service trainees at a college in Poland. As there were not enough places for trainees to do their teaching practice in lower primary classes, they were placed in kindergarten groups to teach English. This new situation provided an excellent opportunity for both the participants on teaching practice and their college trainer to implement action research projects. Trainees documented their own learning and teaching experiences and wrote their theses on their own findings. This chapter describes both the process and the outcomes.

2.   Background to study

The teacher training curriculum for pre-service teacher education contains a methodology course with a component of teaching English to young learners (YLs). This involves a semester of psycho-pedagogy (thirty hours), a semester of YL EFL methodology (also thirty hours) in the second year of a three-year programme. In their third year, trainees are expected to teach young learners (aged 7-10) in lower primary school classes. Teaching practice lasts for a year and it is organised in such a way that trainees teach a class one lesson per week and they observe a lesson taught by their trainee partner. In schools they either co-operate with the teacher of English working with the group of learners: they have one or two lessons with him/her and one with a peer or with a regular class teacher. In the case when their mentor is a lower primary school teacher, trainees integrate the foreign language with the general curriculum.

Trainees are supervised by a trainer who observes and assesses them at least twice a semester. Trainees are required to write a syllabus for every semester and to submit a teaching practice journal at the end of each semester. The trainer is responsible for providing feedback and assessing both the syllabus and the journal. On top of teaching, observing young learner classes, planning the lessons and assessing young learners' progress, trainees are expected to write a diploma thesis as an action research project with young learners. They are asked to identify a problem they face in their teaching, search the literature on the topic, and develop and implement solutions in practice.

Feedback on teaching practice is collected by using interviews, questionnaires, tests, diary entries, observation notes and discussions. In the year 2004/05 there were more students than places in schools; therefore, a group of trainees were allocated to a kindergarten to teach two groups of 5 year olds and two groups of 6 year olds for half an hour twice a week. This situation created not only new challenges, but also new opportunities to develop trainees' teaching skills and to examine how they manage their new tasks.

Since it was difficult to find literature on teaching English to preschool children, trainees were encouraged to find resources they had access to: texts dealing with developmental psychology (Schaffer, 2004) and pedagogical aspects of very young children's education (Klim-Klimaszewska, 2005), as well as writings concerning aspects of attention and concentration, the use of music, play and movement (Brzezińska, 1995; Hannaford, 1995; Smoczyńska-Nachtman, 1992b). Trainees were also advised to consult books not specifically focused on English (Reilly and Ward, 1997) and popular books for parents on educating preschool children in literature designed for parents (Gruszczyk-Kolczyńska and Zielińska, 2005).

3.   Aims of the study

The study aimed to assist trainees in making the best of their teaching practice in kindergarten. This involved helping them develop special skills necessary to teach 5 and 6 year olds, and design and implement action research projects facilitating the process of teaching very young learners. The one-year experience in kindergarten was also used to contribute to improving the teaching of English to YLs component in the methodology course.

The study aimed to find answer to the following questions:

- How do trainees manage to attract and maintain preschool children's attention?

- How do they adjust tasks to meet the needs and abilities of very young language learners?

- How do they increase the exposure of children to a second language (L2) in interactions?

- How can the findings contribute to the development of the YL methodology course at college?

4.   Participants

In total, eight trainees participated in the study; they were allocated in pairs to four groups of preschool children aged 5 and 6. All of the trainees were in their third year and had done one year of teaching practice in a high school. Four of them were allocated in pairs to two groups of 5 year olds, whereas the other four were to teach 6-year-old children.

5.   Instruments

Data were collected with the help of classroom observations, informal talks, a questionnaire and a teaching practice journal. The trainer collected the latter after each semester.

6.   Results and discussion

6.1   Observation

The trainer observed all trainees twice a semester and if there were problems in the lessons an additional lesson was also observed. In the observed classes a great deal of unpredictability was experienced, as the activities prepared by the trainees did not always work with children. They were either too abstract (like the use of flashcards) or too demanding linguistically (kids were expected to listen to L2 with little visual support). Some of the teacher trainees managed to adjust their teaching to the age group quickly: they introduced shorter activities accompanied by movement, music and play with few "pen and paper" tasks. They exploited the toys in the classroom and built on the child's familiar environment in designing their tasks. Some trainees used commercially published books with activities for very young learners and storybooks.

6.2   Informal talks

Trainees would often gather in a tiny teachers' room before and after the classes to discuss their experiences with their peers and their mentors. Their talk tended to focus on learners' behaviour and their difficulty in managing it. For example, "5 year olds need to move all the time!" and "After a relaxation activity they may be even more disruptive than without it!" or "They were so disruptive that I felt like leaving the class in the middle of the lesson." Another typical point they discussed related to the activities they implemented and the materials they used. For example, "They just neglected the flashcards I brought for them!" or "After the third story when I wanted to introduce another one they said: 'Oh no, not a story again!'" Their overall feeling about the unpredictable situations is neatly summarised by a trainee's complaint: "They are so unpredictable, you never know what to expect!" Through such informal talks a lot of stimulating ideas were generated and a lot of support was gained from the peer group and these discussions motivated trainees in further teaching.

6.3 A questionnaire: most successful play activities in kindergarten EFL

Trainees were asked to name the most successful activities in their classes and to give the reasons for their choice. The activities were then shared by all trainees to enrich their repertoire of tasks for kindergarten children. Table 1 presents the results: on the left side the name of the activity is given and on the right the reason why trainees found them useful in their classes.

Table 1: Useful activities and reasons for success in the view of trainees

Name of activity	Reasons for success
Hunt for ...	Children can move a lot and they listen carefully to a teacher's instructions about what to bring (different items each time collected from the floor).
The flight of a bumble bee	Children can move a lot as bees with the classical music in the background and when the music stops they are to fly to a different colour flower in various parts of the room.
Spider and flies	Children can move a lot, stopping when spider catches them. Whoever moves has to answer a question – they know the activity from their general kindergarten curriculum.
Doggy, doggy, who's got your bone?	Children chant together and then they answer the doggy's questions individually, they like the idea of passing a soft fluffy bone behind their backs.
Vocalisations	Children love playing with their voice and saying different words in various ways: slowly, quickly, with a high pitch of voice and a low one, loudly and quietly.
Visualisations	Children enjoy listening to relaxation music and to a teacher's description of the scene; they like to imagine and feel it and later recall the words they remember.

Acting out the story "The frog family"	Children enjoy repetition and acting out. They are given paper plates on strings around their necks with different frog family members and they act them out with pleasure.
Throwing a dice	Children like using the objects available in their kindergarten environment. A dice has pictures of toys on each side. When thrown, kids enjoy answering what is on top and at the bottom.

6.4   Teaching journals

After each semester trainees submitted their teaching practice journals on the description of their group, their aims for the learners and teacher development aims, their syllabus containing a lesson-by-lesson division of the material, forms of assessment, lesson plans with trainees' reflections on them, and a summary. These journals provided useful information on the process of trainees' growth. Here is a quotation from one of the trainee's summary:

> I got used to the volume of the learners' speech, which is always slightly above the level of 'normal'. At the outset, I treated each shout or loud reaction as a way of impeding the flow of my thoroughly prepared lesson. I tried hard to maintain discipline in a school-like way. After some time, I learnt not to pay so much attention to the silence in the classroom. Moreover, I even understood that the more they speak and react to certain stimuli, the better. I don't need all the learners to listen to me simultaneously and I don't care if one of them detaches from the group for the sake of flying birds outside the window. I know they need this freedom of movement and if they don't pay attention, it does not necessarily mean they don't respect me. They might be tired or unhappy, and I cannot force them to behave like puppets according to the script written before the lesson. One may always change the activity if that's more beneficial for the learners.

6.5   Trainees' projects

The eight trainees used a variety of instruments to collect data for their action research projects. Observation and diary turned out to be the most frequently used instruments in conducting their action research projects. Four trainees interviewed their learners and three distributed a questionnaire for other teacher trainees and general kindergarten teachers. In what follows, a short overview is given to the research questions.

6.6   How trainees attract and maintain very young learners' attention

The problem of attracting children's attention was experienced by all trainees and it was most difficult for them to manage. They tried various ways to find out what worked best. They used an instrument (a rattle or a tambourine) or they played the piano to interest the pupils and focus them on the task. They also prepared many short activities for each lesson to change the pace quickly and not allow the learners to get bored. On the other hand, when an activity attracted the children's interest for a longer period, they allowed them to play it. While reading a storybook they would modulate their voice, use facial expressions and realia to involve the children in the listening.

They prepared some attractive materials for the learners in arts and crafts activities so that they were willing to work with them. They introduced a lot of movement into the classes so that the children were not to sit still but they could be physically active. As they were working with the pupils for the whole year, they learned the names of their learners and used them to nominate the children or to manage them. Four trainees used a puppet or a toy to attract the attention of the pupils. They always started a lesson with a song or a chant to signal the beginning of English and to discipline learners. It appeared from one of the trainee's observations that children tended to abandon the activity if the instructions were long and complicated, and when there was nothing to keep their interest. Realia and other props were very useful and rarely failed to attract the children. They had to be physically involved in the activity to maintain their interest in it. Here is a quote from the action research paper of a pre-service teacher working on the use of storytelling:

> The learners enjoy it most when the teacher makes an extra effort to involve a considerable amount of mimicry, vocalisation, gesticulation and tone alteration while telling a story. Children like to be actively involved in the activity, rather than being just the spectators. They take pleasure in imitating the teacher and in being asked questions while the teacher reads a tale.

She also made an observation that in order for the children to sit quietly while listening to a story they have to have movement in pre-listening activities. From the teacher trainees' experience, the most effective attention getters are both visible and audible at the same time. They tended to clap hands in order to attract pupils' attention. Children were easily involved if they were to guess what happened next in a story or in an activity. The element of surprise and unpredictability was found stimulating for children's active participation.

6.6   Matching learners' needs with task qualities

In trainees' experiences, playful activities known to the children encourage them to take part in them. An example of such an activity was "Doggy, doggy who's got your bone?" Other activities used a game children were familiar with from their general curriculum, but this time it happened in L2: in "Chodzi lisek koło drogi" children sing a song or a chant in English, "Incy wincy spider", or a game "Jawor, Jawor, jaworowi ludzie" (London Bridge is falling clown) is familiar to children from their play with peers.

Puppets provided an effective means of drawing and maintaining young learners' attention ensuring a safe and enjoyable atmosphere in the classroom. Trainees developed special activities for "taking English away" from the pupils for the lesson by putting it into a box and closing it for the time of the English class or by driving it away from the classroom in different types of vehicles. The use of music allowed them to use almost exclusively the target language. Instructions delivered in L2 had to be supported by demonstration, gestures, flashcards, realia, intonation and body language to facilitate comprehension. The trainer recalls observing a successful demonstration of the bingo game for the first time to a group of 5 year olds with no Polish instruction at all.

6.7   Suggestions for improving the methodology course

In light of the findings, the methodology course on teaching young learners should be modified in line with the problems teacher trainees faced in the kindergarten. The following topics have to be included in it:

- characteristics of the development of 5 and 6 year olds;
- the role of play, movement, relaxation and music;
- observation of kindergarten classes.

Special attention should be paid to adapting activities for the age group with special focus on movement, designing activities involving play, managing kindergarten children, using the target language for simple instructions supported by body language, singing and chanting without the use of a recording, possibly accompanied by a musical instrument. It is also important to sensitise the trainees to the need to be flexible in teaching very young learners and to respond to their needs and abilities instantly.

7.   Discussion

The trainee teachers identified problems in their teaching situations and they worked on their solutions. They mainly faced difficulties in managing young children and using the L2. They discussed the problems with the kindergarten teachers and searched for the solutions with them. They also exchanged their experience among themselves and supported each other by observing classes, sharing materials and activities as well as filling in questionnaires for each other's research. They were also supported with comments and advice by their trainer. They relied on their own storytelling experience from childhood, the way they were assessed in kindergarten, and one trainee used her musical education, whereas another one applied her daughter's experience in kindergarten.

When children found an activity attractive, they usually got overexcited about it. This resulted in inattentiveness to the teacher's instructions, an immediate switch to L1 and, consequently, falling into a state of uncontrollable euphoria. Usually, in the remaining part of the lesson, the teacher tried to re-establish classroom discipline. It took some time and advice from the trainer and other trainees before the researcher realised that it was not the children who were unco-operative but the approach to teaching them that seemed inappropriate. After a series of classes when the control of children was visibly lacking, the trainee was advised to try to introduce relaxation activities for young children. For example, in such an activity, children sit curled up on the floor pretending to be cocoons with caterpillars inside. Cocoons grow slowly and steadily. Deep breathing is employed. Children gradually stand up in order to fly away as butterflies. Relaxing music is played in the background. This is how one of the trainees reflected on her experience when children did calm down.

> On constructing this relaxation activity I had three things in mind. Firstly, drawing from my experience with introducing a similar activity to children some time during the first semester – children were supposed to lay still and breathe deeply for two minutes, but the activity turned out to be a failure, for they were not able to concentrate on their breathing for so long. I saw a need to weave this activity into a task which would be both meaningful and attractive to them. Secondly, I wanted to relate the activity to the context of the lesson, introduce it in English and make it linguistically productive. Thirdly, I wanted to follow the guidelines for introducing and conducting relaxation activities. One of them says that performing slowed down movements helps children relax.

A problem resulted from the fact that in many cases a class was conducted without the presence of the learners' regular kindergarten teacher. This may have biased the results, since children's behaviour changed considerably in the presence of their teacher. It was easier for the trainee to carry out the activities with the children's regular teacher in the class. At the beginning of the research, she knew that in order to get the children's attention and to make the lessons enjoyable for the learners, it is essential to find activities that are adjusted to the children's level of cognitive, linguistic and physical development. Their choice was also connected with a permanent search for materials suitable for the age group. Drama activities were successful in getting the children's attention when most of the group was involved in acting out and participating actively in the activity. This is how a trainee commented on such a task: "What I wanted to do was to make children move and play and I've got the feeling that somewhere I lost one of the main objectives, namely learning English. In the heat of the lesson, I forgot to elicit some vocabulary and structures from the children whenever possible."

A trainee noticed that although instructions are an inevitable and necessary part of every lesson, they may present no value if not listened to by the group or listened to by only a few children. Learners do not exactly know what they are supposed to do, are confused and either lose interest in the activity or become disruptive. It was difficult to provide any instructions or explanations if pupils' attention was directed to something else (toys or group mates). According to the observations, it is very unlikely for the instructions themselves to arouse children's interest. Signals drawing learners' attention to the teacher and showing them that something new is about to begin come in handy during transitions. The use of a rattle as her established signal was found an effective signal of the change in activity.

A typical problem experienced by trainees was how to elicit from the children English words and phrases as they generally showed preference for non-verbal responses. A problem was also observed rooted in children's natural willingness to play on their own with self-made puppets. It was in several cases extremely difficult to involve children after making puppets and to discipline them in order to utilise their energy in activities imposed by the teacher. It was understandable that the children were reluctant to cease to participate in the activities in which they expressed their personalities and used their skills in a free way and to replace them with pseudo-play, the rules of which were dictated by the teacher.

8.   Conclusions

The kindergarten experience had a lasting effect on the trainees as well as on the trainer and the methodology curriculum. The eight trainees co-operated closely not only in the pairs they were allocated to, but also with the regular kindergarten teachers and they developed a cohesive and co-operative team, exchanging ideas and supporting each other in various challenges encountered in this context. They realised that in order to teach very young children they had to be flexible and act according to what happens in class more frequently than with older learners. They became creative in using kindergarten games, resources and materials to meet the needs of the children. They searched through alternative ways of teaching the children with the help of movement, music and relaxation. They also learned how to conduct a lesson without a coursebook. The trainer also gained a lot from their experiences and the students' projects and published an article on the kindergarten research projects (Szulc-Kurpaska, 2005). One of the trainees also wrote up her project and got it published in a journal for teachers (Bochen, 2005).

The findings were exploited in a workshop conducted for trainees in new location in Poland, and additional topics were introduced on child development at preschool age and their implications for methodology in the third year of college education. This new content was appreciated by college trainees, as more and more often they teach this age group. As a further step, the methodology course on teaching English to YLs will include ways of teaching very young learners and an observation project will also be included. Thus, the findings of the action research will be recycled into the teacher education curriculum of Polish pre-service teachers.

References

Bochen, K. (2005), "The flight of the bumble bee – Can Korsakov and his friends teach English?", *The Teacher*, 6-7, 22-27.

Brigance, A.H. (1991), *Inventory of early development (birth to seven years)*, North Billerica, Curriculum Associates.

Brzezińska, A.I. (1995), *Dziecko w zabawie i świecie języka* (Children in the world of play and language), Poznań, Zysk i Spółka.

Concari, L., Hirsh, F. and Urrestarazu, J. (1990), *Snip snap*, London, Heinemann.

Gruszczyk-Kolczyńska, E. and Zielińska, E. (2005), *Wspomaganie dzieci w rozwoju skupiania uwagi i zapamiętywania* (Enhancing the development of children's attention and memory), Warsaw, WsiP.

Hannaford, C. (1995), *Smart moves, why learning is not all in your head*, Arlington, Great Ocean Publishers.

Harwas-Napierała, B. and Trempała, J. (2004), *Psychologia rozwoju człowieka. Charakterystyka okresów życia człowieka* (Psychology of human development. Characteristics of stages in human life), Warsaw: Wydawnictwa Naukowe PWN.

Ilg, L., Ames, L.B. and Baker, S.M. (1994), *Rozwój psychiczny dziecka od 0 do 10 lat* (Psychic development of a child from 0 to 10 years), Gdańsk, Gdańskie Wydawnictwo Psychologiczne.

Klim-Klimaszewska, A. (2005), *Pedagogika przedszkolna* (Preschool pedagogy), Warsaw: Polski Instytut Wydawniczy.

Reilly, V. and Ward, S.M. (1997), *Very young learners*, Oxford, Oxford University Press.

Smoczyńska-Nachtman, U. (1992a), *Kalendarz muzyczny w przedszkolu* (Musical calendar in kindergarten), Warsaw, WSiP.

Smoczyńska-Nachtman, U. (1992b), *Muzyka dla dzieci. Umuzykalnienie według koncepcji Carla Orffa* (Music for children. Musical training according to Carl Orff's approach), Warsaw, WSiP.

Schaffer, R. (2004), *Introducing child psychology*, Oxford, Blackwell Publishing.

Super songs. Songs for very young learners (2003), Oxford, Oxford University Press.

Szulc-Kurpaska, M. (2005), "'Chodzi lisek koło drogi' or 'Incy wincy spider?' Teaching English to pre-school children", *The Teacher,* 5 (29), 20-26.

About the author

Małgorzata Szulc-Kurpaska, Ph.D., has been a pre-service teacher trainer at the foreign language teacher training college for seventeen years and an in-service adviser in the Lower Silesia region for eleven years. Her interest in young learners started in 1994 when she began teaching in lower primary classes. This experience resulted in doctoral research on the influence of learner strategy training in 9 and 10 year olds. She is a co-author of a programme for teaching 7-10-year-old learners and a co-author of a coursebook for Year 1, *Sparks 1*, both published by Oxford University Press.

Chapter 4
The self-perception of early education teachers of English

Mariola Bogucka

1.   Introduction

This chapter reports on research into how early education teachers of English in Poland make sense of their profession. The interest in this matter stems directly from my work in both pre-service and in-service teacher training, where for years I have had a chance to observe young teachers at the beginning of their careers and those who have been in the profession for some time. How do early education teachers of English in Polish schools perceive their role and significance? This is the main question I would like to find the answer to.

Recently, choosing teaching as a career has gained new dimensions. As Day (2002, pp. 7-8) claims:

> "Teaching takes place in a world dominated by change, uncertainty and increasing complexity. ... Stability of employment and status have been the hallmark of teaching which traditionally has been regarded as a job for life. Little wonder that the post-modern represents more of a threat than a challenge, or that many are confused by the paradox of decentralized systems, i.e. local decision-making responsibilities, alongside increased public scrutiny and external accountability."

To describe the new aspects of modern life, Bauman coined new phrases: "liquid modernity" (Bauman, 2000) and "liquid life". The fact that everything is in a state of flux makes modern changes both difficult to follow and make sense of: "Life in the liquid modern society is a sinister version of the musical chairs game, played for real" (Bauman, 2006, p. 3).

Contemporary changes have undoubtedly affected Polish education. On the basis of research carried out in 2001 and 2002, Kwiatkowska, a leading Polish educationalist, reveals the steady deterioration of teachers' conditions of work, namely an unfriendly atmosphere among the staff, "unhealthy" competition, a fear of being laid off, dramatically increasing violent behaviour of children and teenagers, and a lack of understanding with families of difficult students. However, teacher training programmes do not prepare trainees to cope with new unfavourable conditions as if teaching happened in a harmonious and idealised world. Summing up, Kwiatkowska claims that teachers in Poland are "the victims of inadequate educational reforms" (2005, p. 118). Strikes and protests organised by the Teachers' Trade Unions (ZNP) in

May 2007 were a rather unsuccessful way of voicing teachers' dissatisfaction with the current situation, not only the financial degradation of the teaching profession.

The same analogy of the teacher as a victim is used by Meighan (1986, p. 39). The author, a sociologist, discusses such aspects of the job as "the possibility of constraint, of limited choices and of imposed conditions of work", which make teaching outside the control of teachers. The strong presence of traditional ways of perceiving school and teaching aggravates the teachers' condition, since one cannot argue with one's ancestors; it is more difficult to get rid of "their ill-conceived constructions than those built in our own lifetime" (Berger, 1963, cited in Meighan, 1986, p . 42). The situation of contemporary teachers does not sound inspiring, thus, the central question for this study is as follows: At a time of uncertainty and ever-present constraints what makes teaching English to children a worthwhile profession?

2.   Background: teachers' beliefs about their profession

According to Williams and Burden (1998, p. 56), "there is growing evidence to indicate that teachers are highly influenced by their beliefs, which in turn are closely linked to their value, their views of the world and to their conceptions of their place within it". Hence, in recent years educational research has investigated teaching from the insider's perspective (Richards, 1998, p. 49) but at the same time researchers have studied the reliability of teachers' opinions about their teaching. They pointed out the discrepancy between teacher talk and classroom practice (Kiss, 2000, pp. 171-172). Williams and Burden (1998) admit that "beliefs are notoriously difficult to define and evaluate" and agree with Argyris and Schon (1974) when they cite that "we usually have to infer people's beliefs from the ways in which they behave rather than from what they say they believe" (p. 56). Nevertheless, the formulated opinions and types of attitudes shown are valuable and provide a good insight into teachers' self-awareness and ability to reflect about teaching. "If the teacher-as-educator is one who is constantly re-evaluating in the light of new knowledge his or her beliefs about the language, or about how languages are learned, or about education as a whole, then it is crucial that teachers first understand and articulate their own theoretical perspectives" (Williams and Burden, 1998, p. 57).

3.   The study

3.1   Aims and research questions

The present paper reports on an exploratory qualitative study of early education teachers of English in Polish schools. It aims:

- to find out what English teachers in early education consider significant in their profession;
- to investigate whether teachers have a shared view of professional values and achievements;
- to find out how they plan their personal and professional development and how they view their career prospects;
- and, finally, to explore how they talk about their profession.

At the same time, the study constitutes an in-service action research project for me as a teacher educator. It aims to find out what impact the analysis of teacher talk may have on the evaluation of teacher training and teacher development programmes.

3.2   Participants

In total, 12 teachers took part in the study; they were selected from a group of 46 teachers who participated in either a teaching English to young learners (TEYL) module of their postgraduate studies or were graduates of a TEYL methodology requalification course. They were all female, aged 26 to 42, teaching in Gdańsk, a city of about 400 000 inhabitants. Of those who took part, 11 teach in state primary schools and one in a primary community school (a type of school which is financially supported by parents).

The 12 teachers interviewed all share the same characteristics:

- they have a degree in early education;
- they have formal qualifications to teach English in kindergarten and lower primary school;
- they have acquired official degrees in the Polish teacher development system;
- they are now mainly employed to teach English, rather than to be class teachers;
- they regularly upgrade their qualifications on INSETT courses;
- they have between five and ten years' experience of working with very young and young learners;
- they have a reputation of being "excellent" teachers according to parents and children.

The interviewed teachers were not trained as English or language teachers in the first place. Originally, they studied early education and were trained to work with young children in the lower years of a primary school or kindergarten. However, the group is representative of teachers in early education in Poland, as a vast majority of teachers employed in Polish state and community primary schools have acquired additional qualifications to teach English. The formal requirements include a successfully completed 280-hour requalification course in the methodology of TEYL and a language certificate equivalent to First Certificate of English. Yet, officially, they are not generalists (class teachers) who teach short lessons of English every day. Because of the shortage of teachers of English in early education the moment requalified teachers gain their new qualifications they are asked to specialise in teaching English to children aged 6 to 12.

3.3   Data collection instruments and procedures

In order to gather the information necessary for the research the following steps were employed: lesson observations, identifying the 12 teachers, designing a set of open-ended questions, recording the interviews and, finally, analysis of the collected data.

Prior to the interviews, the author of the article observed all the teachers in their classrooms over a period of three months between April and June 2006. The main aim of lesson observations was not only to see the teachers in action but also to look more closely at the children's behaviour during the lessons. The research based on a qualitative analysis of 12 interviews was carried out in Gdańsk in June 2006.

The selected teachers felt comfortable when speaking English and hence English was the only language of instruction. They had a good rapport with their learners; they knew their first names and could anticipate and manage their problems. The lessons had a clear learner-centred orientation and engaged the children in creative work, especially arts and crafts tasks. Although English lessons (forty-five-minute slots) are taught only twice a week, the learners responded appropriately and the tasks assigned by the teacher seemed to be a source of pleasure and development for them.

All the interviews were carried out in Polish. Although I prepared a list of questions (see Appendix), each interview was different and followed the natural flow of conversation. All the aspects planned were covered; each interviewee influenced the order of the questions and gave her own focus to the interview. Even though different in form, the interviews were almost homogeneous in their outcome. The quotations are the author's translation of the original utterances. Each interview lasted from one and a half hours to two.

4.   Results

The teachers' answers were grouped into the following sections: teachers' understanding of what makes good successful teaching, what they would like to avoid in the future, views on personal and professional development, opinions about the official system of teacher promotion and, finally, teachers' perception of teaching as a career. These are the points the analysis follows.

4.1   Opinions about good practice

The first question about how teachers understand the concept of good teaching clearly referred to teacher activity, yet for the teachers it served as a springboard for talking about their pupils and their successes in learning English. In a similar way, the next question about their biggest professional success immediately turned into a presentation of success stories featuring their pupils: "Good teaching is motivating for children. It provides children with a feeling that they are doing something useful, something they will be able to apply in the future." In the story which followed the teacher quoted a proud parent of a child who was able to communicate in English during their holidays in Italy.

"Good teaching does not only involve just teaching a new language but even more importantly giving children joy, happiness and satisfaction while learning." The example gave an account of a parent who wanted to find out from the teacher the details of an activity his child had at school because it was so enjoyable that they wanted to do it again at home.

"Good teaching involves making a difference in children's lives." "Good teaching means being able to understand where they [children] are and help them to shape and grow." A story illustrating how, presented a girl who was the teacher's "private student". The girl did not like English or her English teacher at school. After a series of lessons her attitude to both the subject and the teacher changed dramatically. The interviewed teacher commented, "Well, it was my little success .... It was her success, but at the same time it was my success as well. It was our mutual success."

Teachers' professional success is discussed in terms of "being a good, respected teacher". The interviewees did not want to elaborate on how they understood the concept and immediately resorted to talking about their learners: "My students' achievements are mine." "My success is my students' joy of learning. Their success is my success." "A teacher's success is a positive change in other people." As a foundation for successful teaching, teachers stressed the importance of mutual recognition and mutual esteem between learners and their teacher. The interviewed teachers valued feedback from parents, although it was not directly about teaching but stories illustrating the children's achievements and progress. They were very modest when talking about their success as if they wanted to highlight the learners' role in achieving it and underestimate their own.

One of the teachers was appointed deputy director in charge of ELT at her school, but she did not mention it as a success. When asked about it, she did not really want to discuss it. She thought it was just her good teaching and recognition on the part of her head teacher. She finished this strand in the interview by saying, "Now, because of the new post, my teaching load is reduced and I miss everyday teaching, especially the youngest children."

4.2　Fears for the future

What the interviewed teachers feared most was falling into a rut of routine behaviour and monotony. Of the 12 teachers who took part, three contrasted their profession with that of a clerk whose job seems to be the epitome of boredom, mechanical and tedious repetition. Again, just like in the case of "mutual success", special emphasis was placed upon the interdependence of teachers and learners in experiencing classroom activities, "Being bored is totally stupefying, your brain stops working." As another teacher put it, "If I am bored, my students will be bored. If they are bored, they will stop liking me. And because young children study for the teacher they will stop learning."

4.3　Personal and professional development

An interesting aspect of teachers' beliefs about themselves and their profession was the lack of a clear distinction between the personal and professional domains. The teachers were almost puzzled by the question whether they could differentiate between the two spheres of their lives: "My personal life totally overlaps with work at school. All the training I had was directly connected with education. Eighty per cent of my friends are teachers." Even when they discussed free time activity they linked the two: "If I take up yoga, I am more relaxed at home and at work." Another teacher related how her professional development benefited her in her private life, as well. "When I learnt to use computers and the Internet, obviously I used the new skills both at home and at work."

As mentioned before, these teachers regularly take part in various INSETT courses, yet when asked about how they plan their own path of professional development, they admitted that it was not planned in any way and the choice of further training was rather accidental. Unfortunately, the courses offered by local teacher development centres are not as varied as they should be. As a consequence, the interviewed teachers accept what is provided rather than make their choices. Such a situation is not conducive to reflection on one's abilities and competences. The interviewed teachers did not specify any aspect of teaching a foreign language, such as how to become a better storyteller, how to develop students' communicative strategies or how to assess children's language abilities better. None of them mentioned self-assessment of their teaching competences and self-directed teacher development as an alternative path of developing as a professional. In other words, they do not seem to be in charge of their own professional development.

As far as the teachers' perception of the importance or prestige connected with acquiring formal qualifications to teach English is concerned, they did not view it as a significant step in their career. The following response is representative of the teachers' attitude: "I can sing and I can draw. Now I can also speak and teach English. The more things I can do as a teacher the more respected I am by my pupils. Children need teachers who set a good example."

None of the teachers mentioned any issues of modern foreign language teaching, such as, intercultural perspectives or making children aware of differences between their native language (Polish) and English. Teaching English was seen as its technical and methodological aspects: teaching a new song, new words or fun activities that children can enjoy and remember. "When my pupils 'bump into' me years later they start talking about some memorable details from my lessons."

4.4 Opinions about the official teacher promotion system

All 12 teachers expressed a similarly negative attitude to the official teacher promotion system, namely resentment. They resent the formal path of teacher development, as it does not do justice to their true merits: creativity or devotion. Too often it is limited to formal filling of documents or the presentation of meaningless certificates. They also resent their head teachers for their unprofessional supervision and mostly ungrounded criticism, since the majority of them do not even know English.

Another common view is the rejection of the staffroom because it is an impersonal, uncomfortable and "cold" place. It looks and feels like an office whereas it should be cosy and home-like. Only one of the 12 teachers likes the staffroom. Actually, she is the teacher who works in a community school. She claims that the staffroom is very well furnished, but first of all the atmosphere among the staff is friendly.

4.5 Teaching as career

Successful development is by no means viewed as climbing financial or administrative rungs up the career ladder. None of the respondents thought it desirable or prestigious to aspire to the position of head teacher. They view career development in terms of gaining better self-understanding and a quest for constant discovery of something new, a feeling of developing continuously and striving to become a more effective teacher. All of the interviewed teachers claim that it is a profession for people who really want to work with children and obviously not everybody can do the job.

Although the teachers seemed to reject the idea of a career in the popular meaning of the term, they miss both financial and social recognition. A recurring theme in the interviews emerged spontaneously without elicitation: the problem of the media. In the teachers' account the media fulfilled the role of "significant other". The opinions about teachers and the situation at schools presented in the media are not justified, as according to the interviewees, currently the media focus on sensational news and deal with shocking stories. The media, as the most influential opinion-forming body, might change the social perception of the profession by showing examples of good educational practice and promoting the true image of a hard-working devoted teacher.

According to interviewees, the media and the fact that teachers are underpaid are to blame for the decline of the status and authority of teachers in modern society.

4.6   Teachers' language use

The language used by the 12 teachers exhibits common traits. First of all, every interview has a number of emotionally loaded words and phrases, such as "fascinating", "unbelievable", "passionate", "spiritual", "satisfying", "energising", "surprising" and "inspiring". As teachers talk about their job, working with children "offers incredible opportunities", "brings about happiness, freshness, joy and enthusiasm". Children are compared to "an untamed ocean" and the context undoubtedly suggests that the metaphor has positive connotations.

Especially when the 12 teachers talked about the essential values in teaching, the language they used was emphatic not only in the choice of words or grammar structures but also in sentence stress. They referred to the dynamic nature of working with children: "*Every day* is different, unexpected, and challenging" as "it requires developing new ways of addressing their learners' needs". They emphasised the "give and take" nature of teaching: "I'm *learning* from the children *so much*." "As a teacher you inspire pupils and at same time you are inspired." "There is *always* something new you can learn."

The most significant aspect of the discourse used is its narrative mode. The teachers illustrate their thoughts and opinions with stories from their school practice. The stories deal with the influence they have had on their pupils' attitude to learning English and examples of successful, effective teaching. They are smoothly interwoven into the flow of the interviews. They are at the same time the source of reflection on the past, offer order and meaning to their present professional life and project a direction in thinking about the future by providing a point of reference, setting goals and making the future efforts more tangible.

5.   Discussion

According to Day (1998, p. 2), "successful teaching will always demand both interpersonal and intrapersonal skills, and personal and professional commitment. It is a synthesis of the head and of the heart". The discussed interviews support this point. The teachers have gained the recognition of pupils and their parents both thanks to their knowledge, technical and methodological skills and genuine personal emotional involvement. "Effective teachers create learning atmospheres which are cognitively and affectively expanding; learning atmospheres which enable the learner to become a more adequate and knowledgeable person" (Pine and Boy, cited in Williams and Burden, 1997, p. 62), and this process gives meaning to their professional lives.

All the interviewed teachers have a shared view of professional values and achievements. Their teaching is empowered by their passion, creativity and genuine interest in children. Hence, the most significant aspect of being an early education teacher of English in Poland is its humanistic and learner-centred character. However, the main focus for the teachers' efforts is creating conditions for emotionally rewarding teaching. At the same time, new developments in modern foreign language methodology, such as promoting learner autonomy and independence, do not emerge from the interviews.

The interviews provided evidence that the teachers developed mainly narrative modes of thought and when talking about teaching did not show any characteristics of a paradigmatic type (Bruner, 1986, as cited in Klus-Stańska, 2002). Success stories, which feature individual students, seem to organise teachers' understanding of the process of teaching. Constructing logical-scientific arguments, rather than narrative only, could provide grounds for a clearer distinction between the personal and professional domains of teachers' lives. It might also facilitate analysing what happens at school nowadays and planning further teacher development.

A feeling of satisfaction that working with children provides makes social recognition seem unimportant and less desirable. However, there is a lack of internal consistency in the way teachers talk about their profession; on the one hand, they appreciate the intimate and private aspect of their work most, whilst, on the other, all the interviewed teachers express their disappointment with the decline of their status and the lack of recognition in society. In addition to this controversial assessment of their own perception, teachers take any criticism of the profession and other teachers personally.

The interviews clearly indicate areas of teacher confusion: although they are proud of carrying out an important mission and seem to find fulfilment, they suffer because of low social recognition. However, the interviewees did not make any attempt to suggest why the media and society might be so critical of teachers.

The world around us is constantly changing: new technologies have offered new prospects and new, attractive sources of knowledge, modern consumerism have tipped the balance between material and spiritual values. Hence, it is not surprising that nowadays society has different expectations of teachers (Day, 1998; Kwiatkowska, 2005). Yet, the way the interviewed teachers perceive their role and significance is rooted in the previous epoch and reflects values which society finds less important. Teachers seem to be locked in a vacuum. They dream about the traditional concept of authority and a high and unquestionable status. The fact that they are needed in a "different way" surpasses their traditional understanding of the profession.

For the time being, private success stories and pleasant memories make it possible to survive the hardships. Generally, in the teachers' talk about their profession the present mingles with the past and the future is seen as an emotionally loaded project aiming at "better, more effective teaching". However, better teaching is not specified in any way.

6.   Implications for future studies

As for what impact the analysis of teachers' interviews may have on the evaluation of teacher training programmes, it enables teacher trainers to identify areas of teachers' professional knowledge which need to be introduced or explored further. However, it is not possible to generalise any of the findings. It is also necessary to study in detail not only the contents of the programmes but also the way they were delivered.

It would be interesting to research the difference in the perception of their profession between early education requalified teachers and early education specialist teachers of English. It might be hypothesised that specialists having studied a more subject-oriented teacher training programme may have a different teaching focus and a different way of talking about their profession.

The discussed interviews concerned only teachers of ten to fifteen years' standing. Exploring the perception of their profession at the onset of their career and years later might cast more light on the possible paths of teacher development. Additionally, another implication of teachers' talking about teaching involves offering other teachers opportunities for sharing experiences, success stories and considered opinions based on school practice in order to facilitate teacher self-understanding and professional development.

References

Argyris, C. and Schon, D.A. (1974), *Theory in practice*, San Francisco, Jossey-Bass.

Bauman, Z. (2000), *Liquid modernity*, Cambridge, Polity Press.

Bauman, Z. (2006), *Liquid life*, Cambridge, Polity Press.

Day, C. (1999), *Developing teachers,* London, RoutledgeFalmer.

Kiss, C. (2000), "Words are but wind, but seeing is believing: do the expressed attitudes of primary EFL teachers reflect their classroom practice?", in Moon, J. and Nikolov, M. (eds.), *Research into teaching English to young learners*, Pécs, University Press Pécs.

Klus-Stańska, D. (2002), "Narracje w szkole" (Narratives at school), in Trzebiński, J. (ed.), *Narracja jako sposób rozumienia świata* (Narration as a way of understanding the world), Gdańsk, Gdańskie Wydawnictwo Psychologiczne, pp. 189-220.

Kwiatkowska, H. (2005), *Tożsamość Nauczycieli* (Teacher identity), Gdańsk, Gdańskie Wydawnictwo Psychologiczne.

Meighan, R. (1986), *A sociology of educating*, London, Cassell Educational Ltd.

Richards, J.C. (1998), *Beyond training*, Cambridge, Cambridge University Press.

Williams, M. and Burden, R. (1997), *Psychology for language teachers*, Cambridge, Cambridge University Press.

Appendix: Questions used to elicit teachers views on teaching.

1. What is good teaching?

2. What is your greatest professional success?

3. What would you like to avoid in your professional life in the years to come?

4. How do you plan your professional development?

5. Are personal development and professional development equivalents for you?

6. Did you consider acquiring the formal qualifications to teach English as a form of professional promotion?

7. What is your opinion about the official system of teacher promotion?

8. What is your attitude to the formal accountability system?

9. Is it possible to have a career as a teacher?

About the author

Mariola Bogucka is an experienced teacher of English and teacher trainer. She works as a senior lecturer at the Foreign Language Teacher Training College of the University of Gdańsk in Poland. Since 1994 she has co-ordinated a regional INSETT project set up to help teachers of English working in all types of schools at different levels to develop professionally. She is co-author of a video course for teachers *Observing English lessons*, published by British Council Stadium UG (1999) and of two language courses for young learners, *Your English ABC* (1999) and *Friends* (2002).

Chapter 5
Story-based language teaching: an experimental study on the implementation of a module in three European countries

Marina Mattheoudakis, Katerina Dvorakova and Katalin Láng

1.   Introduction

This paper presents the results of an experimental study on the implementation of a story-based module in three European countries. The aim of the study was to design story-based input that can be integrated within the standard syllabus for the teaching of foreign languages to young learners. The input proposed was tested with our student teachers who were involved in a series of tasks and experienced story-based teaching both as learners and as teachers. They were further required to reflect on their experiences and provide us with comments and feedback regarding the effectiveness of the input. The paper presents the results of student teachers' implementation of the input in three countries, and discusses their answers to the reflection tasks. In an attempt to explore the similarities and differences in the three educational contexts, we found that the structured input had a significant impact on student teachers' performance. Due to their exposure to the same input sessions, there were several similarities in their presentations. However, we also found important differences and these should probably be attributed to differences in the educational background and culture of the participants.

The educational value of stories and their impact on children's affective, cognitive and linguistic development have triggered foreign language teachers' interest in their potential as a learning tool in the L2 classroom. Literature on the use of stories and picture books in young L2 learners' classrooms has been abundant as educationalists are interested in developing techniques and activities suitable for the particular target group (Brewster, Ellis and Girard, 2002; Ellis and Brewster, 1991, 2002; Garvie, 1990; Jones Mourão, 2006, among others).

This paper was motivated by the authors' interest in the use of storytelling in teacher education. Thus, it proposes a story-based module for student teachers of young foreign language learners and reports on its impact on student teachers' implementation of a story-based lesson plan. The study was carried out by each one of the authors in their respective countries: Greece, the Czech Republic and Hungary.

2.   The theory behind the practice

Narratives and storytelling form part of the oral tradition found in all cultures. According to cognitive psychologists, narratives are used to frame our experiences (Schank and Abelson, 1995) and in this sense they function as schemata which help us organise and interpret our experiences and thus make sense of the world (Lugossy, 2006). With reference to the young language learner, this means that early and systematic exposure to stories will help children "enrich" their schemata but also interpret new information and experiences.

Storytelling has important benefits for children's affective development. Brewster, Ellis and Girard (2002, pp. 186-187) have suggested that children tend to identify with story characters and thus become personally involved in the plot. Storytelling tends to provoke emotional reactions, such as laughter, sadness, disappointment, anticipation and this helps children develop both socially and emotionally.

The use of narratives and storytelling in the L2 classroom has also important benefits for children's linguistic development. Brewster, Ellis and Girard (ibid.) claim that storytelling can create ideal learning conditions since it provides comprehensible input. The meaningful and comprehensible input provided by the use of stories activates the language acquisition device and promotes language acquisition, as learners become able to induce language elements from the data they receive (Krashen, 1981, 1993). Although the comprehensible input is a necessary condition for L2 acquisition, it may not be sufficient. Interactionist theories (Larsen-Freeman and Long, 1991; Swain, 1999) support that learners need to engage in post-listening or post-reading tasks and language-related activities in which they talk and write about what they have listened to or read (Renandya, Rajan and Jacobs, 1999); such activities can make the story more comprehensible but also help learners move from the receptive competence needed for listening and reading to the productive competence necessary for talking and writing (Renandya and Jacobs, 2002). Stories can actually be the stimulus of a wide variety of language-related activities and allow teachers to introduce or revise vocabulary and structures.

Additionally, listening to stories provides young learners with the opportunity to become aware of the rhythm, intonation and pronunciation of L2. Although results of studies on the advantages of starting young with foreign languages are inconclusive, research on the factors affecting foreign accent in a L2 points to the importance of starting young for the development of listening skills and the acquisition of L2 pronunciation (Piske, MacKay and Flege, 2001). Walsh and Diller (1981) suggested that there may be a neurological basis for "difficulty" in eliminating foreign accents after childhood. With respect to the acquisition of suprasegmental features in L2, Tahta and Wood (1981) observed that the ability to replicate intonation dropped rapidly from 8 to 11, while the ability to replicate pronunciation declined more gradually between the ages of 5 and 15. Such findings underscore the importance of using storytelling in young learners' classrooms as this provides them with the opportunity to be exposed to the segmental and suprasegmental features of the foreign language at an early age. In this context, of course, it is important to consider teachers' level of language proficiency as it is not clear yet how teachers' non-native oral skills influence children's pronunciation (Nikolov, 2000).

3.   Why are we not all using stories in YL classrooms?

Given the advantages of storytelling, one may wonder why it is not widely used in young learners' classrooms. According to Ellis and Brewster (2002, p. 1), teachers' resistance to the use of storybooks in young EFL classrooms is mainly due to their lack of confidence in their ability to tell stories or read them aloud. Of course there are also several foreign language teachers who have not been specially trained to teach young learners and are either not aware of the true value of using storybooks or unsure of how to use them.

Teachers' reluctance to use storytelling may also be due to their personal beliefs about teaching and learning. An important source of these beliefs is teachers' own experience as language learners (Richards and Lockhart, 1996, p. 30). The fact that in most European countries – with the exception of the former Soviet Union – the practice of teaching foreign languages in the primary school started twenty or twenty-five years ago which means that the majority of practising teachers in those countries today did not have the opportunity to start young; thus, it is not possible for them to make references to personal learning experiences as young learners and tend to model their teaching on the basis of their own teachers. If such lack of previous learning experience is coupled with insufficient training for teaching young learners, it is no surprise if teachers ignore or underestimate the educational potential of alternative teaching resources, such as storybooks, and opt for materials and methods that are better suited for older learners.

4.   The study

4.1   Aims and research questions

This paper reports on the results of a study in three European countries within the framework of the TEMOLAYOLE project at the European Centre for Modern Language. The aims of our study were:

- to design four forty-five-minute sessions on story-based instruction to young learners;
- to present this input to student teachers in the three participating countries;

- to enable student teachers to adapt a story of their choice and practise telling it in a controlled environment;

- to develop reflective tasks which would allow them to analyse their teaching experience; and

- to examine the relationship between input and implementation, namely, to explore the choices student teachers made when asked to put theory into practice and draw comparisons among participants in the three countries.

The main focus of our study was the impact of the structured input on student teachers' choices during the implementation stage and the similarities and differences found among the three groups of participants (Czechs, Hungarians and Greeks). Thus, we expected to find answers to the following research questions:

(a) Which storytelling techniques and guidelines did student teachers employ during their presentation in order to support pupils' understanding?

(b) What were the similarities and differences in student teachers' presentations in the three countries?

(c) How did student teachers view their story-based teaching? What were the similarities and differences in their answers to the reflection tasks?

The answers to the questions above were provided (a) through observation of student teachers' presentations and (b) through an analysis of their answers to the reflection tasks. The instruments used in data collection were observation, video recording and reflective tasks.

The paper will first make a brief presentation of the structured input and the tasks assigned to our student teachers. Secondly, we will evaluate student teachers' story presentations and discuss their answers to the reflection tasks. Thus we will be able to explore the similarities and differences in the three educational contexts. We expect that the structured input will have a significant impact on student teachers' performance and therefore there are likely to be similarities in their presentations due to their exposure to the same input sessions. However, we also expect to find several variations which will be related to differences in the educational background, context and culture of the participants. Finally, it is expected that student teachers' answers to the reflection tasks will indicate various levels of self-awareness and different attitudes towards learning and teaching.

4.2   Participants

In the Czech Republic, the project was carried out at the Faculty of Education, University of South Bohemia in České Budějovice, in the academic year 2005/06. The participants, 11 in total, were fifth-year students training to become primary school teachers with a specialisation in English as a foreign language. In the text we will be referring to the Czech student teachers as C1 to C11. The project was implemented within their mandatory ELT methodology course in their final year of study. By that time, the participants had already attended two and a half semesters of methodology, one semester of children's literature and one and a half semesters of supervised teaching practice at primary school.

In Hungary, six student teachers (H1-H6) from the Vitéz János Roman Catholic Teacher's Training College in Esztergom participated in the project. They were enrolled in a four-year pre-service teacher training programme to become general classroom teachers with a specialisation in the teaching of English to young learners. At the time of the research, the spring semester of 2005/06, they were in the third year of their studies, having done two semesters of methodology and one semester of children's literature. They had experience with English lesson observation, micro-teaching and English language teaching to young learners at the practice school affiliated to the college.

In Greece, the project was implemented in the spring semester of 2005/06, when the 10 participating students were in the 3rd or 4th year of their studies (G1-G4) They had already completed three semesters in methodology of language teaching and one semester in teaching practice. All of them had attended at least two other elective courses related to English language teaching (for example, micro-teaching, materials evaluation, early foreign language learning and teaching). An important difference between Greek participants and the other two groups of student teachers is that the former are not primary school teachers but are qualifying to become English language teachers in either primary or secondary education. Greek student teachers presented their stories either in threes (G1, G2) or in twos (G3, G4)

4.3 The story-based input

The input sessions were designed by the three authors using the resources listed in the bibliography. The aim was to combine theoretical background underlying story-based teaching with practical tasks which would engage student teachers in practising some of the skills needed. At the implementation stage, each instructor slightly adapted the planned input to suit the particular needs of her class as well as his/her teaching style. The input sessions included the following thematic areas:

- rationale for using stories with young learners;

- types of stories for children;

- criteria for selecting a story;

- adaptation of a story;

- guidelines and techniques for successful storytelling;

- demonstration of techniques by teacher educator.

Due to space limitations, in this chapter we are only going to make a brief presentation of the guidelines and techniques.

4.3.1 *Storytelling guidelines*

Once the teacher has selected and adapted the story, the question is how he/she can present it effectively to young pupils. Guidelines represent steps which can be taken mainly before telling the story and act as story warmers or facilitate setting the stage. Respecting them can help to make storytelling more authentic and enjoyable. The following guidelines and techniques were presented to the student teachers:

- help pupils to realise that it is story time;

- prepare the pupils for the language of the story;

- prepare the pupils for the content of the story;

- help the children to focus on the subject;

- incorporate music, songs or rhymes;

- relate the story to other subjects and make cross-curricular links, if possible.

4.3.2 *Storytelling techniques*

Incorporating storytelling techniques adds a lively dimension to the narration but, most importantly, provides support to pupils' understanding. By storytelling techniques, we understand the steps that can be taken during the narration to maximise learners' comprehension of the story:

- narrate slowly and clearly, allowing time to think;

- vary the pace, tone and volume of your voice;

- make eye contact with the children;

- use visual aids – puppets, masks, pictures and real objects;

- use mime, gestures and sound effects;

- pause where appropriate to add dramatic effect;

- give your pupils sufficient time to look at the visuals and draw their attention to them;

- mix mother tongue and English;

- involve pupils in storytelling.

4.4   Procedure

The first step was the selection of a story from the prescribed list. It was possible for more student teachers to select the same story so that different possibilities of presentation could be seen. Alternatively, two or three participants could work on and present together the same story. The student teachers had two weeks to adapt their story to a primary school level and prepare the narration.

From the list of suggested stories the Czech student teachers selected the following: *The gingerbread man* (C1, C11), *The lion and the mouse* (C2 and C3 as a joint presentation, C7), *The three little pigs* (C5, C10), *Little Red Riding Hood* (C6, C8), *The little red hen* (C9) and *Winnie the witch* (C4). In Hungary, the student teachers opted for *Rumpelstiltskin* (H1), *The three little fiends* (H2), *Little Red Riding Hood* (H3), *The enormous turnip* (H4), *Goldilocks and the three bears* (H5) and *The coyote and Columbia* (H6). Although Hungarian student teachers had the list of recommended stories, they were allowed to choose any story they liked. As already mentioned, Greek students presented their stories in threes (*The whisperer* (G1) and *Itchy-itchy chicken pox* (G2)) and in pairs (*One bear at bedtime* (G3) and *Winnie the witch* (G4)). They actually chose to present the story as well as the lesson plan. All the stories were presented and video recorded in one day. The audience consisted of fellow classmates, which obviously created a different atmosphere in comparison to a real classroom situation.

4.5   Results and discussion

4.5.1 Storytelling guidelines and techniques

The first research question aimed to find out which of the storytelling guidelines and techniques presented in the structured input were used in student teachers' presentations. As some of them (for example, preparing the pupils for the language of the story) could only be incorporated into the lesson plan and not into the actual presentation, the following analysis takes into account only observable features.

Table 1: Guidelines and techniques employed by Czech student teachers

	C1	C2	C3	C4	C5	C6	C7	C8	C9	C10	C11
Helps pupils to realise that it is story time	√	√	√	√	√	√	√	√	√		√
Incorporates music, songs or rhymes	√	√	√	√			√				√

Employs slow and clear narration		√			√	√	√	√	√	√	√	
Uses voice variations	√	√	√	√	√	√	√	√	√	√	√
Maintains eye contact	√	√		√	√	√	√	√	√	√	√
Uses visual aids	√	√	√	√	√	√	√	√	√	√	√
Uses mime, gestures and sound effects	√	√	√	√	√	√	√	√	√	√	√
Pauses to add dramatic effect		√			√	√	√	√	√			
Gives time and attention to visual aids		√	√	√	√			√	√	√	√	√
Involves pupils in storytelling				√					√	√		√

The results show that in none of the three countries did participants choose to mix mother tongue and English. On the contrary, all the participants succeeded in employing voice variations, visual aids, mime, gestures and sound effects. This may be attributed to the fact that they are used to working with these techniques in their teaching practice and they are well aware of their benefits. Especially with respect to visual aids, there was a vast array, including puppets on a stick, finger puppets, flashcards, real gingerbread, realia, a large backdrop painting, and face masks.

All but one student teacher in the group managed to find a way of signalling to their learners that it was story time and maintained eye contact. They used a bell, a magic hat, a musical instrument and special costumes. As far as incorporation of music, songs or rhymes is concerned, music was used in five stories. In *Winnie the witch*, the student teacher created her own magic spells, for example, "Abracadabra, you know what I mean. Abracadabra, let Wilbur is green." The grammar mistake in the magic spell was the only drawback of an otherwise highly successful presentation.

Adjusting the pace of narration to the young learners' needs was one of the main difficulties encountered by the Czech participants. Student teachers who narrated too quickly were, in most cases, also unable to pause for dramatic effect. Even though they presented to fellow classmates and not to real pupils, four student teachers managed to involve their audience effectively (for example, by asking comprehension and prediction questions or eliciting the names of animals on flashcards).

Table 2: Guidelines and techniques employed by Hungarian student teachers

	H1	H2	H3	H4	H5	H6
Helps pupils to realise that it is story time						
Incorporates music, songs or rhymes	√		√			
Employs slow and clear narration		√	√	√	√	√
Uses voice variations	√	√	√	√	√	√
Maintains eye contact	√	√	√	√	√	√
Uses visual aids	√	√	√	√	√	√
Uses mime, gestures and sound effects		√	√	√	√	
Pauses to add dramatic effect			√			
Gives time and attention to visual aids	√	√	√	√	√	√
Involves pupils in storytelling	√	√		√		√

All Hungarian student teachers were able to employ visual aids successfully, maintain eye contact and alter their voices to present different characters and feelings. The use of visual aids turned out to be one of the strongest points of the presentations in Hungary.

In order to involve the audience, some student teachers asked questions regarding the content of the story or encouraged predictions regarding its plot; one student teacher encouraged the audience to participate by asking them to count along with her. H3 who presented the story of *Little Red Riding Hood* chose an extract from *Peter and the wolf* by Prokofiev as background music to enrich the text with the sounds of the forest.

Even though the presentation of H6 was slow, due to her weak language skills (poor pronunciation and grammatical mistakes), it was not clear or well-understood.

Table 3: Guidelines and techniques employed by Greek student teachers

	G1	G2	G3	G4
Helps pupils to realise that it is story time			√	√
Incorporates music, songs or rhymes				√
Employs slow and clear narration			√	√
Uses voice variations	√	√		√
Maintains eye contact	√	√	√	√

Uses visual aids		√	√	√
Uses mime, gestures and sound effects	√	√	√	√
Pauses to add dramatic effect				√
Gives time and attention to visual aids			√	√
Involves pupils in storytelling	√		√	√

There were significant differences in the quality of the Greek student teachers' presentations. In the case of G1 and G2, the narration was fast and the student teachers did not pause to facilitate understanding or add dramatic effect to their reading. Moreover, they did not attempt to create a storytelling atmosphere. A much larger variety of techniques was observed in the presentations of G3 and G4. In order to help pupils realise that it was story time, G3 used a teddy bear whereas in the G4 student teachers wore a hat. Only G4 employed background music in order to create a storytelling atmosphere.

Three of the four groups prepared visual aids in order to help pupils understand the story or particular lexical items but their selection and use varied. Some of them used flashcards, some brought realia and others used miming and gestures.

4.5.2 Similarities and differences

The use of stories in young learner classrooms is rare in the educational contexts of all three countries. Although learners of English may be as young as 5 or 6 years old, teaching follows quite a traditional methodology and working with stories is a marginal rather than a regular activity in young learner classes. As it follows, participating student teachers had essentially no experience of story-based learning and teaching either as learners or as teachers.

In spite of this drawback, all student teachers succeeded in implementing at least four out of the 10 recommended storytelling techniques and guidelines. Looking at the results in all three countries, 9.5% of student teachers used up to four techniques and guidelines, 66.5% of them used between five and eight, and 24% used nine or 10. While in the Czech Republic and in Hungary there were no cases of fewer than four different techniques, two of the Greek groups employed only four techniques. It proved very difficult for them to integrate story-based teaching techniques in their own repertoire, to understand how they can support learning and use them effectively for the promotion of their pupils' linguistic and cognitive skills. Although they seemed very happy and satisfied with the theoretical input provided, they found it difficult to use it in practice during their presentations. The fact that Greek student teachers are not primary school teachers and therefore have not been especially trained to teach young learners might partly explain their difficulties in coping with the tasks.

4.5.3 Reflection tasks

Research suggests that micro-teaching, self-observation and reflection have an immense value in and should be an inseparable part of any educational context (Gebhard et al., 1999; Gwyn-Paquette and Tochon, 2002; LaBoskey, 1993). The literature on reflection does not seem to provide a definition which would embrace all features of this term. In Selby's review (1999, pp. 133-134) several attempts are provided by theoreticians, researchers and educators. Thus, a reflective act has been characterised as "a cyclical process of creating knowledge through transformation of experience" (Kolb, 1984, cited in Selby, 1999, pp. 133-134); it "requires open-mindedness" (Dewey, 1933, cited in Selby, 1999, pp. 133-134) and "involves the creative construction of an autonomous practitioner" (Calderhead and Gates, 1993, cited in Selby, 1999, pp. 133-134). Gilpin (1999, p. 111) summarises five essential components of a reflective activity as follows:

1. noticing, that is, becoming aware of some discrepancy, and observing;

2. reasoning, that is, articulating what has been observed, and analysing it drawing on a wide knowledge base;

3. change of some kind, whether conceptual or practical;

4. questioning of whatever has hitherto been taken for granted;

5. affective involvement.

In practice, reflection tasks allow teachers to analyse the teaching process, to reconstruct their knowledge and to adapt their practice to their students' needs. Similarly, reflection tasks enable learners to develop a critical mind, to take responsibility for their own learning and to develop more effective learning strategies.

In this project, reflection tasks were designed and delivered to student teachers upon completion of the implementation stage (that is, adaptation and presentation of the story). Reflection tasks were planned in accordance with the structured input, and aimed to elicit student teachers' reflections about whether they managed to (a) establish a storytelling atmosphere, (b) adapt the story, (c) provide suitable context, introduce the characters, link the story to the learners' experience, (d) prepare learners for the language of the story, (e) make cross-curricular links, (f) offer visual and oral clues, (g) narrate clearly, and (h) encourage participation.

- *Establish a storytelling atmosphere*

Regarding the creation of a storytelling atmosphere, Czech participants' answers to the reflection tasks indicate that they were aware of its importance during their presentations and used a great variety of techniques to signal the start of story time and make their audience motivated and attentive (namely, sitting in a circle on the carpet, playing a tune, ringing a bell, using background music). The answers of the Greek student teachers, however, do not always agree with the observations made during their presentations. Thus they refer to the use of techniques which were mentioned in their lesson plans, but were not always part of their presentations. Hungarian student teachers, on the other hand, seem to be aware of the fact that they did not cater for the creation of a storytelling atmosphere.

> G4: "A special storytelling atmosphere in the classroom was established to help pupils to relax and focus on the subject by the background music, by using pictures, puppets, posters and some prompts."

> G2: "We didn't plan to go with the students to a special corner in the classroom. We would just announce that today is story time … our students would be relaxed just because it would be story time and they love it!"

> G1: "… having a soft, background music … was to help students to feel the mystery and the romance of the story …."

> H4: "... the atmosphere was familiar. The seats were in a circle, so everybody could see the board and could concentrate."

- *Adapt the story*

Czech student teachers seemed to be more sensitive and concerned about adapting the story to the learners' ages and proficiency level than the other two groups. They practised some self-criticism and also suggested possible improvements: for example, "too brief in some parts", "the adult audience is very different from children", "'I am caught in this trap' should be modified to 'I am in this trap'."

Most Greek and Hungarian student teachers stated that they found no specific reason for adaptation and attributed their decision to various factors: the age and level of their pupils, the simple language of the story, the limited length of the story and the children's familiarity with the story.

Contrary to the rest of the group, two Greek student teachers gave account of several changes they made. They explained or simplified unknown words, replaced unfamiliar words with familiar ones (for example, "furious" with "very angry"), deleted words, shortened the length of the story, split long sentences or added sentences for better organisation.

- *Provide suitable context, introduce the characters, link the story to learners' experience*

Czech and Greek student teachers reported that they used various techniques in order to promote those aims and activate "learners' existing schemata" (G1). However, once more, Greek participants' answers mostly refer to the content of their lesson plans rather than to the actual presentations. Czech student teachers' comments show a better understanding of what they actually did during storytelling

- *Prepare students for the language of the story*

Czech and Greek student teachers' answers indicate awareness of the importance of preparing learners for the language of the story. In particular, they stated that they revised known words, elicited key vocabulary by using picture word cards, used posters and handouts, crosswords and visuals.

The majority of the Hungarian participants did not prepare the audience for the language of the story, and referred to their lesson plans:

> H2: "I didn't prepare them for the language of the story, but I planned it in my first lesson plan."

> H5: "On story presentation I didn't prepare my students. For me the main aim was the storytelling and the pictures, the presentation."

These statements show that Hungarian student teachers had a different focus in their minds; they put emphasis mostly on the presentation and not on the adaptation of the story.

- *Make cross-curricular links*

Czech student teachers mentioned several school subjects (Czech, music, biology, natural science, civics, art, PE) as areas where they managed to establish links with English. One of them exemplified it by suggesting making a gingerbread man as an art activity. Both Greek and Hungarian student teachers seemed to be a bit challenged by this task. This was manifested in the following statements:

> G3: "I think there weren't any opportunities for cross-curricular links."

> G2: "The story could provide the opportunity of making cross-curricular links with the subject of biology or anthropology, however, the level of the students did not allow the teacher to do much. For this reason we only focused on the body parts included in the story as well as on a brief discussion on children's illnesses."

> H5: "There were many opportunities which I didn't explore."

> H6: "I've tried to make cross-curricular links with the North-American natives' legends. That's why I have chosen this tale, but I didn't talk about the natives."

It is interesting to note that Hungarian student teachers suggested various cross-curricular links in their lesson plans which, however, they did not actually implement during their presentations.

> H3: "In my lesson plans I made exercises about animals."

> H4: "If I could make my plans again, I would make an agricultural part of the lesson … is it possible for the turnip to be enormous?"

- *Offer visual and oral clues*

All participants expressed their satisfaction with the variety of visual and oral clues they used. Regarding the oral clues, they mostly chose to change their tone of voice, employed intonation for dramatic effect and put emphasis on word and sentence stress.

- *Narrate clearly*

Of the Czech participants, eight were satisfied with the clarity and speed of their narration. The others stated that they could have spoken more slowly, clearly and loudly. Half of the Hungarian student teachers expressed discontent, and provided suggestions and improvements.

None of the Greek student teachers expressed dissatisfaction with their narrating skills:

> G2: "We tried to adopt a slow rate of reading, which, combined with the use of mime and pictures, made our narration comprehensible and interesting."

> G3: "We read the story slowly and some parts we acted them out: thus it was understandable and straightforward."

- *Encourage participation*

Most Czech student teachers reported that they did not invite the audience to participate in their presentation. Only one participant suggested that she "could have invited the audience to sing along".

As for the Greek participants, they all reported that they applied some kind of technique to enhance involvement. In particular, they reported that they invited their audience to suggest alternative endings to the story, or involved them in a discussion (as a pre-listening activity), employed jump-up cards (as a while-listening activity), asked them to design the cover of the book or retell the story in rap music (as post-listening activities).

Prediction and open questions were the most common techniques used by Hungarian student teachers. H1 mentioned that although she invited the audience to participate orally, they failed to repeat the rhyme. On the whole, Hungarian participants noted that they did not involve their audience in their presentation.

Summarising the results of student teachers' answers to the reflection tasks, participants claimed that they were for the most part successful in offering visual and oral clues, in narrating clearly and in encouraging peer participation. However, they felt that they were not equally successful in making cross-curricular links between English and other school subjects, or in adapting the story to students' age and proficiency level.

Regarding the similarities among participants in the three countries, the majority of student teachers stated that they encountered difficulties in the preparation of story-based teaching and pointed out that though rewarding, it was also very time consuming. They also found it difficult to perform in front of an adult audience which is vastly different from an audience of young learners. Finally, they all stressed that the recording made them more nervous and felt that this affected their performance.

Hungarian student teachers, in particular, expressed their concerns about their weak linguistic competence which probably affected their performance. On the other hand, Greek student teachers who seemed to have serious problems with the use of storytelling techniques during the presentation did not express any concerns about the difficulties they actually encountered. Such lack of awareness probably points to the insufficient teaching practice those students receive and ultimately to their lack of teaching experience with young learners.

5.   Conclusion

Although the input provided to all student teachers in the three participating countries was identical, students' presentation of the stories and the implementation of the guidelines and techniques varied significantly. In the light of our findings, we feel that several suggestions can be made in order to improve the story-based input, and thus enable trainers of student teachers to optimise their material and story-based syllabus.

In particular, it is important for the trainer to adjust or modify the input according to student teachers' educational background and context. For example, Greek student teachers who are generally exposed to more traditional teaching approaches may need to have more practice in story adaptation and presentation. Also, it is necessary to provide student teachers with an adaptation task before the actual presentation. Story adaptation is quite demanding and student teachers should practise as much as possible. To this aim, for example, student teachers may be required not only to adapt but also compare different adapted versions of the same story.

With respect to the story presentation, it might be helpful for student teachers if they have access to video demonstrations of other student teachers or practising teachers who use storytelling techniques in their classrooms. Watching other teachers following and implementing the guidelines and techniques provides them with a model and facilitates understanding of the task required. With reference to the reflection activity, it is advisable to separate reflection tasks on story presentation from the respective ones on lesson plans. It might also be preferable to use open-ended questions in order to elicit detailed responses rather than a "yes" or "no" answer. Finally, trainers should be flexible and open to student teachers' suggestions (for example, students working in pairs on one story, or different people selecting and presenting the same story). It is important to acknowledge and encourage student teachers' creative powers and allow them space to experiment, discover and innovate.

References

Brewster, J., Ellis, G. and Girard, D. (2002), *The primary English teacher's guide*, England, Penguin.

Ellis, G. and Brewster, J. (1991), *The storytelling handbook for primary teachers*, London, Penguin.

Ellis, G. and Brewster, J. (2002), *Tell it again! The new storytelling handbook for primary teachers*, London, Penguin Longman.

Garvie, E. (1990), *Story as vehicle*, Clevedon, Multilingual Matters.

Gebhard, J.G., Hashimoto, M., Joe, J. and Lee, H. (1999), "Microteaching and self-observation. Experience in a preservice teacher education program", in Gebhard, J.G. and Oprandy, R, *Language teaching awareness. A guide to exploring beliefs and practice*, Cambridge, Cambridge University Press, 172-184.

Gilpin, A. (1999), "A framework for teaching reflection", in Trappes-Lomax, H. and McGrath, I. (eds.), *Theory in language teacher education*, Harlow, Longman, 109-118.

Gwyn-Paquette, C. and Tochon, F.V. (2002), "The role of reflective conversations and feedback in helping preservice teachers learn to use cooperative activities in their second language classrooms", *The Modern Language Journal*, 86, 204-225.

Jones Mourão, S. (2006), Understanding and sharing: English storybook borrowing in Portuguese pre-schools", in Enever, J. and Schmid-Schonbein, G. (eds.), *Picture books and young learners of English*, Munich, Langenscheidt, 49-58.

Krashen, S. (1981), *Second language acquisition and second language learning*, Oxford, Pergamon.

Krashen, S. (1993), *The power of reading. Insights from the research*, Englewood Colorado, Libraries Unlimited.

LaBoskey, V.K. (1993), "A conceptual framework for reflection in preservice teacher education", in Calderhead, J. and Gates, P. (eds.), *Conceptualizing reflection in teacher development*, London, Falmer Press, 23-38.

Larsen-Freeman, D. and Long, M.H. (1991), *An introduction to second language acquisition research*, London, Longman.

Lugossy, R. (2006), "Shaping teachers' beliefs through narratives", in Nikolov, M. and Horvath, J. (eds.), *UPRT 2006: empirical studies in English applied linguistics*, Pécs, Lingua Franca Csoport, 329-352.

Nikolov, M. (2000), "Issues in research into early FL programmes", in Moon, J. and Nikolov, M. (eds.), *Research into teaching English to young learners*, Pécs, University Press Pécs, 21-48.

Piske, T., MacKay, I.R.A. and Flege, J. (2001), "Factors affecting degree of foreign accent in an L2: a review", *Journal of Phonetics*, 29, 191-215.

Renandya, W.A., and Jacobs, G.M. (2002), "Extensive reading: Why aren't we all doing it?", in Richards, J.C. and Renandya, W.A. (eds.), *Methodology in language teaching*, Cambridge, Cambridge University Press, 295-302.

Renandya, W.A., Rajan, B.R.S. and Jacobs, G.M. (1999), "Extensive reading with adult learners of English as a second language", *RELC Journal*, 30 (1), 39-61.

Richards, J.C. and Lockhart, C. (1996), *Reflective teaching in second language classrooms*, Cambridge, Cambridge University Press.

Schank, R.C. and Abelson, R.P. (1995), "Knowledge and memory: the real story", in Wyer Jr., R.S. (ed.), *Advances in social cognition. Volume VIII*, Hillsdale, Lawrence Erlbaum Associates, 1-85.

Selby, G. (1999), "Assessing reflection in the pre-service practicum", in Trappes-Lomax, H. and McGrath, I. (eds.), *Theory in language teacher education*, Harlow, Longman, 133-145.

Swain, M. (1999), "Integrating language and content teaching through collaborative tasks", in Ward, C.S. and Renandya, W.A. (eds.), *Language teaching: new insights for the language teacher*, Singapore, SEAMEO Regional Language Centre, 125-147.

Tahta, S. and Wood, M. (1981), "Foreign accents: factors relating to transfer of accent from the first language to a second language", *Language and Speech*, 24 (3), 265-272.

Walsh, T.M. and Diller, K.C. (1981), "Neurolinguistic considerations on the optimum age for second language learning", in Diller, K.C. (ed.), *Individual differences and universals in language learning aptitude*, Rowley, MA, Newbury House, 3-21.

About the authors

Marina Mattheoudakis is an Assistant Professor at the Department of Theoretical and Applied Linguistics, School of English, Aristotle University of Thessaloniki. She holds an MA in TEFL from the University of Birmingham, UK, and a Ph.D. in Lexicology from the Aristotle University ("Problems related to Greek-English lexical loans"). She teaches courses in second language acquisition and language teaching methodology at both the undergraduate and graduate levels. Her current research interests are in second language acquisition, teaching methodology and teacher education (training and development).

Katerina Dvorakova works as a lecturer and teacher trainer at the Faculty of Education, University of South Bohemia in České Budějovice, Czech Republic. She specialises in methodology of teaching English to young learners. She also supervises teaching practice and teaches practical language and communication skills courses. Together with a colleague, she is working on a series of locally published English textbooks for Czech lower secondary learners. In terms of research, her main area of interest is Waldorf pedagogy with a particular focus on teaching foreign languages at primary level, which is also the topic of the Ph.D. dissertation she is currently working on.

Katalin Láng is an EFL teacher and teacher trainer at Vitéz János Roman Catholic Teacher's Training College, Esztergom, Hungary. Her professional experience includes teaching children and adults (both pre-service and in-service education), teaching methodology, children's literature, as well as doing lesson observation and mentoring. She is currently pursuing her Ph.D. studies in applied linguistics at the University of Pécs, Hungary.

Chapter 6
Authentic picture books in the lives of young EFL learners and their teachers

Réka Lugossy

1.   Introduction

This chapter looks at how children between the ages of 7 and 10 and their teachers benefited from a reading project in four Hungarian primary schools, where children have no access to the target language outside the classroom. The reading materials were authentic picture books used in the class to supplement the English as a foreign language (EFL) syllabus. The children could also take the books home to read and share them with siblings and parents. In the first part, I will look at theoretical assumptions which support the use of stories in education, in particular in the foreign language lesson. I will consider the role of narratives in cognitive, affective and social development, as well as their implications for the development of language and literacy. This is followed by the presentation of the empirical research, and the discussion of findings. I will report on the effect of in-class and home reading of picture books on children, their teachers and their close communities. The issues of involving boys and providing equal opportunities through using authentic picture books are also discussed.

2.   Narratives as educational experiences in EFL

2.1   Cognitive development

Narratives affect human existence in various ways. One of these ways is what is referred to as cognitive development. Schank and Abelson (1995, p. 1) claim that "all human knowledge is based on stories constructed around past experiences". Therefore, stories function as schemata on the basis of which we make sense of the world. From the point of view of its implications for cognitive development, the schemata theory suggests that if we expose children to stories we provide them with more opportunities to interpret new information and gradually develop "disembedded", more abstract ways of thinking. In Margaret Donaldson's (1987) view, this is the prime function of education.

2.2 Developing identity

Beyond the scientific understanding of humans as biological beings, there is a perspective that deals with the development of humans as social and spiritual beings, who are ultimately constructed in and by narratives (László, 2005a and b). From this perspective, a fundamental tool in humans' search for meaning is telling and listening to stories. Bettelheim (1991, p. 3) claims that by reading fairy tales we learn to understand ourselves and others, and learn to "relate to them in ways which are mutually satisfying and meaningful".

A function of narratives which links the personal with the collective, and thus helps the shaping of both, is that narratives create social bonds. As Horsdal (2006, p. 5) remarks, "we are building communities while we narrate". That narratives forge relationships by their intimate sharing is supported by descriptive studies of story-therapies, in which participants learn to provide and accept support from one another, gain confidence and courage, and ultimately make sense of their lives through telling and listening to stories (King and Nikolov, 1992). Betty Rosen (1988, p. 118) also documents how long-term exposure to myths and other deep impact narratives affected comprehensive schoolboys' self-expression, it helped them come to terms with themselves, while at the same time provided opportunities for the teacher to know her students better, and construct her identity as a teacher.

2.3 Language and literacy development

The idea that narrative patterns facilitate understanding and remembering (Elley, 1989, p. 176) gains particular importance in the language classroom, where through stories children may acquire words and structures in contexts that are relevant to their lives. Elley (1989) documents that children process the language at deeper levels if the focus is on meaning, rather than form: that is to say, they tend to remember more from stories than from contrived exercises, especially when narratives can be related to learners' lives. This is in tune with Donaldson's (1987) findings which show that childhood learning in general, and language learning in particular, occur in a meaningful context which children can relate to their own experience.

Alongside the opportunities for learning language in a meaningful and motivating context, sustained exposure to narratives greatly contributes to awareness of print and thus promotes literacy in the long run. Heath (1994, p. 75) shows that children growing up in mainstream communities "learn certain customs, beliefs, and skills in early enculturation experiences with written materials". A salient example in this sense is the labelling activity, as it trains children very early in the initiation-response-feedback cycle, which they will later on encounter as a basic interaction pattern of classroom lessons. In this context the bedtime story becomes a major literacy event in that it prepares preschoolers for displays of knowledge expected in school. Studies also suggests that repeated exposure to stories promotes the development of the language style used in stories (Rosen, 1988), as well as children's background knowledge of a variety of topics (Purcell-Gates, 1989, cited by Bialystok, 2001, p. 158).

2.4   Building on narratives in the curriculum

Considering the benefits of telling and listening to stories and "thinking in stories", one would think that creating and cultivating narrative sensibility (Bruner, 1996) is a main priority in education. However, narrative as a mode of thought is valued differently in different cultures. Bruner (1996) distinguishes between paradigmatic and narrative thinking, and points out that most Western thinking predominantly focuses on the rational functions of the mind, and tends to dismiss the value of imaginative and affective learning experiences. Consequently, the convention in most schools is to regard narrative as decoration (Egan, 1989) instead of exploiting its potential as a means for cognitive development.

3.   The study

In the following I will present research on a reading project involving children and their teachers in four primary schools in Pécs and surrounding areas. While there have been previous attempts to involve young EFL learners in extensive reading programmes in the county (Bors, 1999), the present project is special thanks to the quality of authentic reading materials which were both used in class and which the children could borrow and share at home.

The materials are authentic picture books, "written for children's enjoyment and enrichment" (Dunn, 1997, p. 1), with no specific language teaching aim. There are books for young children (Old Macdonald) and books slightly older learners appreciate more (The big blue sea, Coral goes swimming). Also, knowing how the early classroom readings may influence boys' and girls' attitudes to reading (Hall and Coles, 1999), special attention has been paid to choose books for both girls' and boys' interests (for example, The big red bus is usually welcomed by boys, while Cats sleep anywhere is preferred by girls).

The books also vary in the different styles of illustrations as well as in the range of techniques including watercolours, crayon, embroidery and collage. Also, many of them contain elements that encourage the children to have hands-on experience with the books (flaps to lift, mirrors to look in) and challenge the teachers to involve the children in story reading. Because of the attractive layout and interesting content (also important from a cross-curricular point of view), children encounter language embedded in contexts that make sense to them, and this makes language learning a natural and holistic experience in the classroom setting. The books were selected and generously donated by Opal Dunn, expert on young learners and initiator of several

REALBOOK projects for bilingual children and young learners of EFL worldwide. The teachers participating in the project also receive Realbook News, a newsletter edited by and published by Opal Dunn (www.realbooks.co.uk), containing an annotated book list as well as a feature article on a relevant topic related to real books in the lives of children.

3.1   Research questions

I intended to find answers to the following research questions:

- How does using authentic picture books at school and at home influence children's and teachers' motivation?

- How do story reading and interaction influence pupils' and teachers' linguistic development?

- How does the use of books influence (1) peer co-operation, (2) teacher-student rapport, (3) co-operation between teachers and (4) co-operation within the larger community (for example, parents and teachers, siblings)?

- How does reading in L1 and L2 interact?

3.2   Participants

The four teachers involved in the project were graduates of the University of Pécs, where they had previously participated in courses related to story-based teaching. While all of them showed interest in using stories in their classes, they did not have the ambition to use authentic materials before the project. The reason for this was that they did not have access to books they found appropriate in terms of language and content for young learners.

The teachers were selected in a way so as to present a variety of educational backgrounds both in terms of the students taught, as well as in the individual differences among the teachers themselves. Thus, two of them (T1 and T2) were former Russian teachers who received their English teaching degrees after participating in a three-year retraining programme in 1996. T1 teaches in a village school where English is not regarded as a prestigious subject, and where most children come from disadvantaged sociocultural backgrounds. Based on previous observation, T1 appeared to be less confident in her abilities as an English teacher, and more motivated in making her pupils interested. On the other hand, T2 was confident in her teaching, while at the same time she appeared in need of materials and teaching techniques for young learners. As informal feedback gained from her pupils also suggested that her lessons were quite boring, our hidden agenda was to increase her motivation and encourage her to develop more awareness as to the needs of young learners.

T3 and T4 were, at the time of the project, recent graduates of our university. They both teach in fairly popular and acknowledged primary schools in Pécs. They have a good rapport with the children, and are professionally very well prepared. In these schools the children come from a middle-class background with a relatively print-rich environment. All the teachers used picture books with several groups of children aged 7 to 12.

3.3   Procedures

The experiment started in the academic year of 2000/01, and is still going on at all four settings. Teachers were provided with a set of 20 authentic picture books that they read regularly together with the children during the English class. An extra set of books was provided so that the children can borrow. Borrowing is not compulsory, but teachers try to introduce and work with the books in a way so as to raise children's attention and encourage their reading for pleasure.

In order to collect information about the processes and outcomes of the project, qualitative techniques were used. We relied on teachers' self-observation schemes, teachers' diaries, classroom observation carried out by external observers, and semi-structured interviews with the teachers at the end of each school year.

4.   Results and discussion

As I presented the findings in terms of attitudinal, motivational and linguistic development at length elsewhere (Lugossy, 2006a), I will only consider these points briefly, and discuss some of the issues which, although originally not focused on in the research questions, emerged in the course of the project, and indicate areas for further research. Such is the case with (1) the potential of picture books to provide equal opportunities for culturally deprived children, and (2) their power to involve boys in cases when other teaching materials do not. Finally, I show some unexpected turns in the project.

4.1   Attitudinal and motivational outcomes for children

According to all four teachers and the external observers, the children look forward to storytelling in the English class and they are happy to take part in it. "It's a totally different atmosphere," says T3 in the first interview, "it doesn't feel like a lesson at all, it's like story telling and they love it." The teachers' comments in this sense suggest that stories are not associated with learning, and therefore create a natural environment crucial in child language acquisition (Krashen, 1985; Nikolov, 2002). At the same time, the comment implies that "usual" lessons are not really considered interesting either by pupils or by their teachers.

Children also gladly borrow the books, which, unlike their textbooks, are attractive and interesting, and non-compulsory. According to the teacher from the socially disadvantaged school (T1), "some of the children have never in their lives seen books of this quality, and maybe they never will". Apart from the sensational aspect of the books and of the event of sharing stories in the classroom, the children's enthusiasm is also explained by the successful reading experience. Due to the usually short and easy-to-understand texts and the illustrations the children understand what they hear and read.

As for the children's motivation to read, it appears that they read more in English than beforehand. The question whether the project will influence their motivation to read in Hungarian as well naturally cannot be answered. However, it is encouraging to see the children bring in some of their own Hungarian books and ask the English teacher "to read them together in English" (T1 and T3). Children's self-initiated engagement in literacy-related activities is good news in terms of their attitudinal development. On the other hand, it is also crucial that teachers respond appropriately to these suggestions, and thus create the shared understanding of literacy as a cognitive and social process (Hudelson, 1994; Smith, 1985).

4.2   Attitudinal and motivational outcomes for teachers

Using real books in the classroom had brought about changes in teachers' professional lives on different planes, motivation being one of them. All the teachers were enthusiastic about the books, and showed interest in dealing with them right from the beginning. However, due to differences in age, personality and background, they appeared to adopt somewhat different attitudes to using them in the classroom.

Young and enthusiastic, both T3 and T4 found pleasure in experimenting with books, and perceived it as a challenge: "Anytime we start reading a new book," says T3, "I rack my brains for something interesting to do with it." This sounds promising in the sense that the excitement of taking risks with new materials in new ways is believed to prevent routinisation and the disenchantment that sets in towards the later stages of teachers' careers (Huberman, 1989, cited by Rudduck, 1992).

At the beginning of the project, T1, less confident, less energetic and possibly more tired than the younger teachers, appreciated the books partly because she found they provided opportunities to relax both for herself and her pupils. As the project progressed, T1 seemed to have grown more conscious about what she could achieve with the help of the books, saying that "I wouldn't have believed there are so many opportunities in these books."

4.3   Peers, siblings and parents

The positive influence of real books goes beyond the participants of the project. In the first interview, T1 recalled how children started asking their teachers to use similar books at the German lessons. Also, the siblings of the pupils participating in the project have access to the books at home. Therefore, they often stop the teachers on the corridor saying "I love the book you read out in my sister's class." In a survey investigating children's reading choices, Hall and Coles (1999) identify a positive relationship between the amount of reading done by children and living with siblings who read a lot. The same survey also pointed out peers' influence on children's reading choices and habits. In this sense the project may be beneficial not only for the participant students, but also for the children who are in touch with the participants.

Another interesting point relates to the parental involvement. Teachers' reports suggest that parents in the rural school are more responsive to the teacher's efforts and more supportive of the Real books project. This is in tune with Burstall's (1980) findings in the sense that in small schools pupils tend to form closer relationships with their teachers and subsequently develop positive attitudes towards learning. In our case it is the relationship between parents and teachers that can be compared in the two schools, with parents in the village school being closer to the teacher and therefore more explicitly responsive than parents in the popular school, who only meet the teacher on formal occasions and rarely give any feedback.

4.4   Linguistic outcomes

At the end of the first year of the project, T1 commented: "I wouldn't have dared to use this kind of books on my own ... I would have thought they were too difficult for my students." This is a frequent worry teachers share in connection with using authentic materials: because their language is not explicitly tailored to foreign language learners' needs, we fear that these books may turn out to be too challenging linguistically for pupils.

However, the teachers claim that the children have acquired a lot of new words and structures from the books (without being threatened by an eventual word test). Teachers' diaries present evidence for what teachers articulate in the interviews: rhythmic patterns are easily acquired and remembered for a long time. All children remembered "Can you spot the spotty dog?", although the text is full of words that are not among the most commonly taught ones. When T3 revised the book after a while, she found that children "could recall all the difficult expressions at once, like slippery snake, prickly hedgehog, furry mole and jet black cat". She attributed the children's successful recall and their ability to use these words in new contexts to the memorable linguistic and visual context.

4.5   Group dynamics

Teachers claim to have developed a more open rapport with their pupils through working with the books: "I feel closer to the children if I tell them a story at the end of the lesson. And they are a lot more open towards me" (T3). Also, teachers report that even those children who tend to be difficult to discipline in the classroom are captured by real books. "There were always one or two children difficult to motivate and to discipline and when I am telling the stories they are simply glued to the books," says T2. I will come back to this point when discussing boys' involvement.

Another advantage in terms of group dynamics was apparent mostly in the village school, where the great number of Gypsy children are not usually accepted by their peers. It is a common experience in Hungarian classrooms that pupils dislike and may refuse to work with Gypsy children in pair and group work. T1 reports that both sharing the stories and doing the follow-up activities have enhanced co-operation in the classroom. In *Whose hat is that*, the main protagonist, a cat, has to repeatedly find his way through the labyrinth and take the hats to different owners. T1 reports successful co-operation during this activity, with the poorest student in English turning out to be the fastest at finding the way. This confirms the teachers' claim that even those pupils who were considered less able by their peers perform well in story-related activities and enjoy reading the books at home. This has increased peers' appreciation for them.

The fact that children could take the books home also enhanced co-operation and autonomy: T1 mentioned that after reading the first book in class she lent it to a child. By the next lesson the book had already been going around, and the children themselves kept track of who had it and who was going to take it next.

4.6   Providing equal opportunities with picture books

Findings suggest that while the books were greeted with enthusiasm in all four schools, the project has had particular relevance in School 1, where learners come from socially disadvantaged backgrounds, and in terms of access to books are at a disadvantage compared with children from other schools. Thus, story reading in the English class and the opportunities to borrow the books provided opportunities for learners who have no or limited access to such learning experiences in their L1.

Heath (1982) shows that children who are socialised into sharing books with adults, and into the routines and discourse of story reading, are likely to be more successful in literacy-related activities at school. Literacy being the key to academic success (Bialystok, 2001), schools need to compensate for what homes cannot offer in terms of promoting literacy development. Integrating authentic children's books in the EFL programme and thus presenting reading as a worthwhile activity may enhance opportunities for academic success in the case of culturally deprived children.

Besides motivational and attitudinal gains (as shown above), using English picture books presents cognitive gains as well. Exposing children to narratives and to the visual input of fine art picture books expands their background knowledge of a variety of topics, and they learn to problematise issues of interest. One of the examples is a comment coming from an 8 year old, who after reading "Noah built an ark one day" said, "I didn't know Noah took two from each species". Understandably, much of the commenting that occurs related to these books happens in the first language, and it takes appropriate scaffolding on the part of the teacher to turn children's comments into opportunities for learning the target language. On the other hand, comments in the mother tongue can be looked at as proof of the thinking process that underlies the shared reading activity.

4.7   Keeping boys interested

The power of authentic picture books to involve boys emerges as a recurrent issue in all teacher interviews and diaries. T1 claims that "not even the boys had to be disciplined" while sharing books. The boys' involvement in story-related activities also comes as something unusual, as they are "not very keen otherwise". All teachers claim that it is difficult to maintain boys' interest as they easily lose patience during activities. However, whenever it came to the reading sessions, boys appeared interested and were able to focus on the books. It is only that during reading "they added their comments to the pictures more loudly than the girls" (T1). This was perceived by teachers as a sign indicating interest rather than misbehaviour.

The boys' interest in this sense needs to be seen in relation to educational experiences across genders. According to Hall and Coles (1999), boys read less than girls, and also have a less positive image of themselves as readers. Due to the predominantly feminine culture of the primary class and language lessons in particular, and to the lack of male role models with respect to reading, boys appear to identify literacy-related activities as a primarily female occupation, with which they find hard to identify, especially in the years of puberty (Hall and Coles, 1999). Millard (1997) also presents evidence for the difference in girls' and boys' experiences of reading and writing, and shows that school promotes versions of literacy which hold more appeal for girls than for boys. This results in boys not being sufficiently engaged in the reading process and, consequently, falling behind, particularly in the language curriculum. Millard (1997) suggests that one of the ways to redress this imbalance is to make sure that both boys' and girls' reading interests are equally provided for. This can be achieved by using intrinsically motivating and cognitively engaging reading materials, as well as a balanced programme of activities for both genders.

As pointed out earlier, the books used in our project were selected so as both girls and boys could find something of interest. Teachers note that while there are common favourites, boys and girls tend to make different choices as to what they would like to read, provided they are given the opportunity to choose. The *Big red bus* comes last on girls' list in School 4, while *The big blue sea,* a meditative book about the fond relationship between the mother and her daughter, is preferred mostly by girls. Boys found the latter book "too girlie", "uninteresting", and with "nothing to laugh at", and therefore they "definitely indicated that they would rather stay out of it for once ..." (T1).

In our project three teachers out of the four (T1, T3 and T4) regularly negotiated the next book to read with the children, and gave them the choice to borrow whichever book they wanted. There is, however, only one documented account of a teacher's inquiring about why boys did not like one particular book (*The big blue sea*). With this question, the students were made to think about the reasons for their preferences, while the teacher obtained valuable information as to the kind of books boys disliked (namely, the ones they perceived to be lacking adventure and humour). The systematic inquiry about why students preferred certain books to others is important not only for the information it reveals in terms of their reading choices, but also, if learners are given the opportunity to make choices in their learning, and are asked to explain these choices, the chances increase that they develop critical thinking, which is, sadly, not a main priority in Hungarian schools. This is yet another area where a sensible EFL programme might compensate for shortcomings in first language education.

4.8   Unexpected stories

Besides the positive results and processes presented so far, there are also other episodes that need to be briefly described for the sake of deeper understanding. One of these relates to T2, who in spite of our encouragement did not read the books regularly. When she did, she kept the traditional frontal arrangement (typical of Hungarian classrooms), claiming that it was easier to "handle the students" like this. This also suggests that the children did not have that many opportunities to use the books in an interactive fashion. Apparently, the efforts to motivate T2 have been less than successful, but at least the participating pupils have seen sources of English other than the textbook and enjoyed stress-free story reading every now and then.

T2 was also reluctant to lend the books, lest "something might happen" to them. Both middle-aged teachers shared this worry, as they perceived the books as something rare and expensive that they would be unable to replace. This is understandable if we consider the fact that all along their teaching years they had been in need of appropriate materials. Compared with their older peers, the younger teachers appear to be more flexible and pragmatic, and focus on providing children with more learning opportunities rather than saving the books from any potential harm.

Another intriguing point refers to why the teachers of other subjects did not grasp the opportunity to use the books in their lessons. I expected that colleagues would want to use these books either for their cross-curricular implications, or simply because they treat topics of human importance (for example, friendship, family relationship, loneliness, physical handicap). As T1 notes in her diary after dealing with All kinds of people (Damon, 1995), a lift-the-flap book depicting people from various species and with various characteristics: "I wish they included something similar in young learners' coursebooks for environmental studies. For example, skin colour seems to be quite an ambiguous issue for Hungarian children." Still, colleagues referred to lack of time as the main reason for not using these books in their lessons. This is in tune with the findings of a study on English teachers' beliefs and practices, which reveals that what teachers articulate as lack of time, basically, relates to their underlying beliefs about teaching and learning, in particular about the educational value of stories (Lugossy, 2006b).

Among the pleasant surprises that the project has given us is the news that several more English teachers started work with the same picture books (either borrowing them from their colleagues who had been involved in the project or from the English Teachers' Resource Centre, where we had also placed copies of the picture books). When I asked one of these unexpected joiners about what made her use picture books in her lessons she told me she had long realised that neither she nor her students had much in common with the textbooks they were using and she wanted to make everyone's life better, including her own.

5.   Conclusions

The findings of the Real books project suggest that both learners and teachers have gained from regularly reading picture books in the lesson and at home. It appears that children are more motivated to learn English, more open towards one another in the English lesson, and show signs of linguistic development. Other findings that emerged relate to boys' successful involvement, as well as to the potential of picture books to provide opportunities for the literacy development of children from unprivileged backgrounds. Finally, teachers also developed a more open and friendlier rapport with their students, and they seem to have grown more conscious about their teaching.

References

Bettelheim, B. (1991), *The uses of enchantment: the meaning and importance of fairy tales* (4th edition), London, Penguin.

Bialystok, E. (2001), *Bilingualism in development: language, literacy and cognition*, Cambridge, Cambridge University Press.

Bors, L. (1999), "An investigation of Hungarian primary school teachers' and pupils' views of the Baranya Reading Project and suggestions for improving the design of the project", unpublished M.Ed. dissertation, University of Leeds.

Boyle, A. and Woolford, S. (1998), *Whose hat is that*, London, Walker Books Ltd.

Bruner, J. (1996), *The culture of education*, Cambridge, Massachusetts, Harvard University Press.

Burstall, C. (1980), "Primary French in the balance", in Holden, S. (ed.), *Teaching children*, London, Modern English Publications, 86-90.

Damon, E. (1995), *All kinds of people*, London, Sadie Fields Productions Ltd.

Donaldson, M. (1987), *Children's minds*, London, Fontana Press.

Dunn, O. (1997), *Realbook News*, 2 (1). Retrieved from: www.realbooks.co.uk on 30 June 1998.

Egan, K. (1989), *Teaching as story telling: an alternative approach to teaching and curriculum in the elementary school*, Chicago, University of Chicago Press.

Elley, W. (1989), "Vocabulary acquisition from listening to stories", *Reading Research Quarterly*, 24 (2), 174-189.

Farjeon, E. and Mortimer, A. (1996), *Cats sleep anywhere*, London, Frances Lincoln Ltd.

Hall, C. and Coles, M. (1999), *Children's reading choices*, London, Routledge.

Heath, S.B. (1982), "Questioning at home and at school: a comparative study", in: Spindler, G. (ed.), *Doing the ethnography of schooling: educational anthropology in action*, New York, Holt, Rinehart and Winston.

Heath, S.B. (1994), "What no bedtime story means: narrative skills at home and school", in Maybin, J. (ed.), *Language and literacy in social practice*, Clevedon, Multilingual Matters, 73-95.

Hindley, J. and Benedict, W. (1995), *The big red bus*, London, Walker Books Ltd.

Horsdal, M. (2006), "Life-story narratives in voluntary organisations". Retrieved from: www.lua.it./esrea/papers/Horsdal.doc on 9 August 2006.

Hudelson, S. (1994), "Literacy development of second language children", in Genesee, F. (ed.), *Educating second language children: the whole child, the whole curriculum, the whole community*, Cambridge, Cambridge University Press, 129-158.

Krashen, S. (1985), *The input hypothesis: issues and implications*, London, Longman.

King, N. and Nikolov, M. (1992), "Story-making and drama with two groups of Hungarian children", *Modern English Teacher*, 1, 1-8.

László, J. (2005a), *A történetek tudománya* (The science of stories), Budapest, Új Mandátum Könyvkiadó.

László, J. (2005b), *A mai pszichológia emberképe* (The human in contemporary psychology), *Magyar Tudomány,* 11, 1366.

Lugossy, R. (2006a), "Browsing and borrowing your way to motivation through picture books", in Enever, J. and Schmid-Schönbein, G. (eds.), *Picture books and young learners of English*, Munich, Langenscheidt, 23-35.

Lugossy, R. (2006b), "Shaping teachers' beliefs through narratives", in Nikolov, M. and Horváth, J. (eds.), *UPRT 2006: empirical studies in English applied linguistics*, Pécs, Lingua Franca Csoport, 313-336.

Millard, E. (1997), *Differently literate: Boys, girls and the schooling of literacy*, London, RoutledgeFalmer Press.

Nikolov, M. (2002), *Issues in English language education*, Berne, Peter Lang.

Puttock, S. and Lambert, S. (2000), *Coral goes swimming*, London, Hodder Children's Books.

Rosen, B. (1988), *And none of it was nonsense: the power of storytelling in school*, London, Mary Glasgow Publications.

Rowe, J. (1998), *Can you spot the spotty dog?* London, Random House Children's Books.

Rudduck, J. (1992), "Practitioner research and programs of initial teacher education", in Russel, T. and Munty, H. (eds.), *Teachers and teaching: from classroom to reflection*, London, Falmer Press.

Schank, R.C. and Abelson, R.P. (1995), "Knowledge and memory: the real story", In Wyer Jr., R.S. (ed.), *Advances in social cognition, Vol. VIII*, Hillsdale, Lawrence Erlbaum Associates, 1-85.

Smith, F. (1985), *Reading*, Cambridge, Cambridge University Press.

Souhami, J. (1996), *Old MacDonald*, London: Frances Lincoln Ltd.

Waddell, M., and Eachus, J. (1994), *The big blue sea*, London, Walker Books Ltd.

About the author

Réka Lugossy is an Assistant Professor at the Department of English Applied Linguistics, University of Pécs (Hungary), where she teaches courses on EFL methodology and use of narratives. Her main interests include children's literature, empirical research into classroom processes and teachers' development.

Chapter 7
German as a second foreign language in Greek compulsory education: curriculum and continuity

Charis-Olga Papadopoulou

1.   Introduction

In the year 2005 the teaching of a second foreign language, German or French, was introduced in Greek primary education, thus extending its compulsory learning by two years. Undoubtedly, this is a positive development and corresponds to the European policy of "mother tongue plus two foreign languages – Starting young". However, research so far has shown that there is cause for concern in relation to continuity in language learning from primary to secondary education. In the case of Greece, the two available curricula for German as a foreign language (GFL) (for primary and secondary education respectively) have been systematically compared and analysed so as to identify any sources of discontinuity. Curriculum has been chosen to be the focus of the study, since it is related to some of the most important factors which either threaten or ensure continuity in language learning. The present paper discusses identified serious overlaps, discrepancies and methodological weaknesses, especially in relation to young learners. Furthermore, it indicates the direction of changes to be introduced in order to ensure continuity. This study highlights the influence of the specific educational context on the aforementioned issues and, therefore, offers – given the diversity of early foreign language learning in Europe – a basis for inter-European comparison.

German has been taught in Greek secondary education for more than ten years. Pupils learn English as their first foreign language (starting at the age of 8, in primary school) and in secondary education they may choose a second foreign language (German or French). In the academic year 2005/06, German was introduced in primary education as well. We are now approaching the end of a two-year pilot phase, whereby German (or French) is taught in the last two years of primary education (when the learners are 10-12 years old). After that, it is the ministry's intention to introduce the teaching of a second foreign language nationwide. There are currently two curricula for German as a Foreign Language (GFL), one for the two tuition years of primary education and one for the three compulsory years of secondary education. The primary education GFL curriculum (PC) was developed in 2005, whilst the secondary education one (SC) was introduced in 2003.

Both curricula (as with all foreign languages curricula in Greece) are part of the Cross-thematic Common Framework of Foreign Languages Curricula. In this framework the overall aim put forward is in tune with basic concepts like literacy, multilingualism and multiculturalism. Activities related to multilingualism and multiculturalism are considered to be necessary, not only in order to promote mutual understanding and respect amongst the nations, but also to help learners develop cognitively and affectively. All activities should, therefore, contribute to achieving the overall aim, that is that learners develop language abilities so as to communicate in various linguistic and cultural contexts (in real-life predictable or unpredictable communicative situations) with the help of linguistic and paralinguistic means. Learners should become aware of the fact that languages are not only a tool for communication amongst people with different ways of thinking and talking, but also a tool for gaining access to and managing information in different fields. Language is approached in a holistic manner and it is regarded as text, as social process and practice, whilst it serves the learners' socialisation.

In the academic year 2007/08 pupils who have had GFL in primary education will enter secondary education and so the question of continuity in their learning arises. The purpose of the research undertaken and reported in this paper was to compare the two GFL curricula, to examine whether and to what extent fears for discontinuity are justified and to propose a theoretical framework of changes in order to ensure continuity.

2.   (Dis)continuity in foreign language learning

There are numerous terms related to the issue of continuity in the relevant literature, for example "bridging the gap", "crossing the bridge", "Übergangsproblematik", "Weiterführung", "Anknüpfung", etc. This, according to Schmid-Schönbein (2001, p. 154) indicates both the lack of clarity or certainty and a common concern for addressing an urgent issue, the lack of continuity, a concern systematically pointed out (for example by Bausch and Helbig-Reuter, 2003, p. 199; Bebermeier et al., 2003; Bludau, 1998; Helfrich, 1999; Mertens, 2001; Piepho, 2001, pp. 347-349; Schuhmacher, 2001, as cited in Steinbrügge, 2003, p. 19; Sauer, 2000, pp. 3 and 5).

Discontinuity may arise as soon as any foreign language is taught in two subsequent educational sectors (primary and secondary education). Discontinuity in foreign language (FL) teaching and learning is a frequently identified problem (see for example, Edelenbos and Johnstone, 1996, for the case of the Netherlands; Gattullo and Pallotti, 2003, for the case of Italy; Low and Wolfe, 1993/1995, as cited in Blondin et al., 1998, for the case of Scotland, etc.). According to Blondin et al. (1998, p. 35), it negatively affects mainly the weaker or slower learners but it also drastically minimises any general advancement that could have been achieved thanks to early foreign language learning.

There are two basic misconceptions related to early FL learning which appear to be central to the problem of discontinuity. The first relates to the idea that early FL learning provides only some additional tuition years to the years any foreign language is taught in secondary education. In contrast, it is often emphasised how language learning in primary education is characterised by a different "learning culture" (Christ, 2003, p. 452), adopts quite different objectives, contents, teaching methodology and approaches to assessment. The second misconception is that early foreign language learning is not "really" learning but amounts to and is restricted to playing and having fun, and it is in secondary education when learning "really" begins.

Although learners are prepared for a changed learning environment in secondary education, they "definitely do not expect that what they have learnt will be questioned or completely ignored" (Lortz, 1998, in Schmid-Schönbein, 2001, p. 154). It is often observed how such misconceptions result in practices which undermine the teaching and learning taking place in primary education. In secondary education, curricula often start from scratch and ignore or fail to incorporate any experiences, knowledge and skills that have been acquired in primary school. Ironically, the best case scenario is that what FL learners have learnt in primary education will be repeated and/or will not be further developed (Christ, 2003, p. 452). The worst case scenario is that this is perceived and experienced by learners as a punishment, and they end up feeling frustrated and with no motivation to carry on with language learning.

Blondin et al. (1998, p. 56) summarise the factors which may cause discontinuity in FL learning as: (a) lack of communication between the two sectors' teachers and other parties involved, (b) incompatibility between the two sectors' objectives and/or lack of specified objectives, (c) diverging teaching methodologies and themes as well as differences in language proficiency of teaching staff, (d) failure to identify and address discontinuity issues in teacher education, and (e) restricted acknowledgement in secondary education of the knowledge and skills acquired in primary education. Out of a wealth of other factors which may also cause discontinuity (mixed-ability classes, teacher attitudes and practices, intervention or lack of guidance on behalf of the ministries, etc.), the present paper focuses on curriculum-related issues, the reason being that some of the most important factors which cause discontinuity as well as some of the most important measures against it can be addressed and implemented through the FL curriculum.

Ensuring continuity in FL learning has, in the last decade or so, become an important goal. Blondin et al. (1998, p. 57) single it out as one of the basic pieces of advice they give and consider it to be a responsibility of practitioners, trainers, headmasters, researchers, academics and politicians alike. In order to ensure continuity in FL teaching and learning, some of the most important measures suggested so far by the European Commission (2003, pp. 16-23, 2004, pp. 15 and 17) include the following:

- development of a common language rationale and identification of specific objectives beyond the boundaries of one educational sector;

- definition of the basic pedagogical principles in the case of early teaching of languages (and cultures);

- examination of the adjustments to be made in primary education curricula;

- introduction of the European Language Portfolio;

- co-operative diagnosis of learners' abilities and competences at the beginning of each sector;

- actions in order to inform parents and society about early FL learning;

- identification of the necessary improvements and changes in teacher education;

- strengthening the communication channels between the educational sectors.

The present paper focuses on the first five measures and, on the basis of the research outcomes, proposes a theoretical framework for a common GFL curriculum encompassing all five years of tuition.

3.   Research outcomes

The research outcomes presented here revolve around the following points of reference and comparison: (a) objectives, (b) themes, contents and activities, (c) assessment, and (d) teaching methodology. Examples of curricular elements which relate to both problematic and smooth continuity from one educational sector to the next have been singled out from both curricula. Table 1 summarises the research outcomes, which are then elaborated and interpreted.

Table 1: Summary of research outcomes

		Discontinuity	Continuity
GFL Curricula	Objectives	Repetition of objectives Objectives not always properly allocated Important elements not included in both curricula	Continuity concerning the overall aim Progression of certain objectives Gradual increase of demands and difficulty level
	Themes, contents, activities	Repetition of themes and activities adopting similar approach Same types of texts, not always appropriately allocated	Progression of activities Systematic introduction and practice of grammar and syntax in the SC
	Assessment	Assessment not properly differentiated or linked	Common general assessment rationale
	Teaching methodology	Certain inappropriate techniques in the PC No interrelation between the two sectors No detailed description in both curricula	Common techniques and activity types

3.1   Objectives

All objectives included in the PC are repeated in the SC in which there are two new objectives, the one related to linguistic awareness and the one related to language mediation. The former objective focuses on the comparison of the German language to the Greek or other languages, and the latter aims to enable learners to take up the role of the mediator in everyday communication settings. All other objectives are repeated in the case of the SC with only minor modifications. To give an example, the PC objective "learners can understand simple texts they listen to" is further specified in the SC by the phrase "… even when there are elements of a dialect in the spoken text". The repetition of objectives is perhaps most problematic in cases of typical objectives for beginners' learning. Thus, given that "learning the alphabet", "getting acquainted with the sounds of spoken German", "learning how to pronounce basic German phonemes/words" and "intonation" are included in the PC, they should not be repeated in the SC. Although it should be noted that their repetition would be appropriate in cases of remedial work. In any other case, such repetitions indicate that the already acquired knowledge and skills are bound to be ignored, which is, as already mentioned, one of the most important factors causing discontinuity. Furthermore, it is not always clearly stated that certain objectives are present in both curricula. For example, speech acts appear to be of importance in both cases, but they form an explicitly stated objective only in the SC This is a representative example of the unsatisfactory clarity of objectives to be frequently noted. In the same line of thought, there is often a lack of balance in relation to the analysis and theoretical underpinning of objectives. Cross-thematic language work, a core element of today's language learning, is analysed in detail and with examples of recommended practice only in the SC. This, given the cross-thematic nature of language learning in primary education, is regrettable. The same holds for the aforementioned objectives of "language mediation" and "linguistic awareness".

Apart from more detailed specifications, objectives are often modified in terms of their operationalisation in the SC. For example, in relation to the PC reading objectives, which are repeated in the SC, it is specified that secondary education language learners may alternatively choose the texts they wish to read. There is, in some cases, a progression to be observed from one sector to the next, in that learners are encouraged to autonomously produce texts (written or spoken ones) or in that they are expected to recognise and identify regularities in the linguistic system(s) or register and style features, (preferably) on their own. Such operationalisation and progression modifications as well as the implementation of the overall aim (set by the Cross-thematic Common Framework of Foreign Languages Curricula) are curricular elements which could contribute to ensuring continuity in GFL learning.

3.2   Themes

The repetition observed as far as curricular objectives are concerned also applies to themes, contents and types of texts. This can be easily explained, since themes, contents and texts are always linked with objectives, whereby the former are the means of achieving the latter. However, it is not basically the repetition itself which would cause discontinuity problems, although the learners' different age and interests would call for differentiations. Themes like "my family" or "body parts" appear in both curricula linked to similar or identical approaches, with no or minor differentiation in difficulty levels, and, therefore, causing discontinuity. It is difficult to avoid learners being bored or frustrated. A way of addressing this problem would be to allocate in the SC more sophisticated or demanding tasks to the same contents, themes or types of texts, aiming to build on previously acquired knowledge. Unfortunately, this does not appear to be the case in the two Greek GFL curricula. In other words, there seems to be restricted, if any, differentiation on the basis of the different learners' age and interests or depending on their progress. In addition, certain types of texts which would be appropriate for the PC only, for example fables, appear in the SC too, and vice versa, texts like information brochures appear in the PC as well.

On the other hand, in some cases texts are properly chosen in terms of their length (word/phrase level in the PC – longer texts in the SC), in terms of the related activities, for example repeated listenings and multiple aids in the PC – fewer listenings and less guidance/help from the teacher in the SC or spelling letters/words/short sentences in the PC – spelling activities embedded in writing activities in the SC. Similarly, verbal responses to texts are not obligatory in the PC activities (at least at the beginning), which is in agreement with early FL learning principles like the silent period, whereas learners are expected to practise several types of speaking tasks in the SC. Finally, grammar and syntax become specific and explicit activities only in the SC, whereas in the PC learners are to be sensitised in relation to the linguistic system, but no systematic practice or theoretical understanding are aimed at. So, in some cases activities have been found to provide a means of achieving continuity in GFL learning.

3.3 Assessment

The general assessment rationale is common in both educational sectors. Assessment is to be continuous, varied, clear as to its criteria, valid as to its outcomes, carried out by teachers and learners alike, and aimed at not only checking learners' performance but at providing feedback for the teaching and learning processes. This general rationale is appropriate and could ensure effective assessment procedures. However, there are certain problems to be noted. Assessment is not properly differentiated according to the different age groups, or the learning and teaching processes. In other words, the same assessment procedures are foreseen in both curricula. This contradicts one of the basic principles of early foreign language learning, namely that grades and formal assessment procedures are often omitted, since, on the one hand, one of the objectives would be to create a friendly, pleasant learning environment for young learners, and, on the other hand, in primary education grades are generally either omitted or differently expressed than in secondary education. Consequently, the inclusion of formal tests in the PC is considered to be inappropriate. Perhaps, this is why the Ministry of Education issued a guideline specifying that no pressure related to grades should be exercised on primary education language learners. This may be a step in the right direction, but without the provision of alternative approaches to evaluation, much is left to be desired. Furthermore, although the concept of self-assessment is mentioned in both curricula, self-assessment or peer-assessment are analysed only in the PC. Similarly, concepts like the dossier or the learners' learning folder are mentioned only in the SC, and it becomes yet again obvious that the two curricula are not fully aligned.

3.4 Methodology

One of the first problems to be identified, mainly in the SC, as far as teaching methodology is concerned (which can be directly related to the aforementioned problems with objectives), is the lack of clarity. Take as an example the objective "learners should actively participate in various learning activities". It is not analysed how this is to be organised, put into practice and evaluated by the teacher. The rationale and the teaching methodology inherent in any objective are unclear or even absent. It can, therefore, be concluded that the SC does not satisfactorily address teaching methodology issues. On the other hand, the features of the desired kind of lesson are described in detail (for example, the introduction of language games or morphology exercises), which, however, taking into consideration the first point made, results in a rather prescriptive curriculum approach. In contrast, the PC provides a detailed account of principles, techniques and approaches, which is positive, but there are problems concerning certain teaching techniques and methodology issues suggested in the PC, and which would be inappropriate for learners aged 10-12 years old. To go into one of the most striking examples, hand-puppets are one of the three techniques suggested in the curriculum, the other two being total physical response and storytelling. Whereas the last two are indeed appropriate and can contribute immensely to both the quality of teaching and learning provided and to ensuring continuity, hand-puppets have been argued to be inappropriate, even for younger learners (see Cameron, 2001, p. 213; Kubanek-German, 2003, p. 86; Mindt and Schlüter, 2003, p. 121), so this is not regarded as an appropriate technique.

A final issue that needs to be discussed here relates to the lack of interrelation between the teaching methodologies suggested in the two curricula. Learners at the end of primary education are not prepared for secondary education in terms of the changed learning activities, ways of teaching and even of assessment which await them. What complicates matters even more, no modified teaching and learning processes are foreseen or suggested in the SC, according to the teaching methodology and the learning processes proposed in the PC. On a more optimistic note, one of the factors which could contribute to ensuring continuity relates to specific activity types and techniques which the two curricula have in common. Projects or language games play an important role in both curricula and these could help learners successfully continue their learning from one educational sector to the next.

4.   The theoretical framework for a common GFL curriculum

Should a common GFL curriculum be appropriate and successful (at least as far as continuity is concerned), there are certain criteria to be met. A common curriculum needs to: (a) be in line with relevant theory and research, (b) be adjusted in the Greek context, and (c) build on those elements of the existing curricula which contribute to ensuring continuity and eliminate or minimise elements found to be problematic. Furthermore, improvement suggestions need to be incorporated, for example in relation to early FL teaching methodology or assessment issues as well as to the link between the two sectors. The main points of the developed theoretical framework for such a curriculum are presented in Table 2.

Table 2. A theoretical framework for the proposed common GFL curriculum

Objectives for all five years of compulsory education (two years of primary education and three years of secondary) need to be defined:

- so as to implement the overall aim;
- so that they all gradually progress;
- clearly and operationalised;
- so as to avoid overlaps and repetitions;
- appropriately allocated;
- on a common basis for all tuition years;
- depending on the learners' age (8-15 years old) and subdivided into two age groups, that of late childhood ("spätes Kindesalter", see Kubanek-German, 2001, p. 156) for learners 8-10 years old and that of puberty years (for learners 10-15 years old). Such a categorisation can be justified on the grounds of not only the learners' interests or behaviour but also their cognitive development and learning styles.

Themes, contents and types of texts should be selected in such a manner that:

- repetitions and overlaps are minimised or, when necessary, a differing approach can be applied;
- they are properly allocated for all tuition years.

Activities should:

- be organised on the basis of the aforementioned objectives, themes, contents and types of text;
- progress depending on the learners' age, interests, knowledge, competences and cognitive development, for example as far as grammar and syntax are concerned.

Following the common general rationale, in the common GFL curriculum, assessment needs to be differentiated and:

(a) in primary education be informal, foster the learners' involvement in the teaching and learning procedures, their learning awareness, their self-assessment and reflection, as well as their autonomy; and

(b) in secondary education include formal assessments techniques but continue to foster the learners' involvement in the teaching and learning procedures, their learning awareness, their self-assessment, reflection and their autonomy.

The two educational sectors need to be linked in relation to assessment, so that both teachers and learners are aware of and build on previous knowledge and learning experiences.

Further activities should be incorporated in all years of GFL learning which aim to diagnose the learners' knowledge and skills, and "traditional", already suggested in the curricula, assessment techniques need to be reconsidered and adjusted, so as to both reflect a more learner-centred approach to evaluation/assessment and to establish continuity across the two sectors.

The European Language Portfolio is one of the most effective tools to, on the one hand, promote autonomous and reflective learning as well as alternative assessment techniques and, on the other, to link the two stages of learning as far as assessment is concerned. Since it is already available (on a pilot basis) for Greek secondary education, it is of outmost importance and, one might add, urgency to develop the respective European Language Portfolio for primary education and link it to the portfolio used in secondary education.

In relation to teaching methodology, the following aspects need to be put forward by the common GFL curriculum.

Firstly, the description provided for all teaching methodology issues should be detailed and clear, since teachers are often left to rely only on the curricular guidelines (for example, when in-service training is sparse or limited).

Secondly, adjustments need to be made as far as the early learning of GFL is concerned. Principles, approaches and techniques which are inappropriate for the specific age group (in the sense that they can be characterised as too "childish") need to be modified, theoretically justified and practically elaborated. In addition, basic features of early foreign language learning, established by previous theory and research to be important, need to be incorporated in the curriculum, for example, listening/speaking before reading/writing, the silent period, formulaic language, processes like (re)noticing-(re)structuring-proceduralising, etc.

Thirdly, in order to ensure continuity, a teaching methodology bridge is suggested. Apart from the focus on common techniques and familiar activity types (storytelling, total physical response), in the last year of primary education and at the beginning of secondary education, the following aims are to be achieved:

- ensure the gradually changing balance of skills;
- support the learners' progression from imitative to cognitive learning styles;
- proceed from practice to theory;
- gradually increase learner autonomy;

- modify the frequency of activity change;

- modify the role of games and music;

- diagnose the learners' transition profile (Rück, 2004);

- provide material packages, in order to address mixed-ability classes (see for example, Low and Wolfe, 1996);

- build on and expand previously acquired knowledge.

5.   The way forward

The present paper presented and discussed the comparison and analysis undertaken for the two Greek GFL curricula. The research outcomes, informed by previous research and relevant literature, served as a basis for the proposed theoretical framework for a common GFL curriculum, which could contribute to ensuring continuity in GFL learning in Greek compulsory education. However, what is mostly needed, in order to proceed in a valid and promising manner, is future research. Research areas which are considered to be important relate to monitoring and analysing the pilot introduction of the teaching of a second foreign language in Greece and its effects on the second foreign language teaching and learning of secondary education. Such areas may include, to mention only a few examples, research foci examining teaching and/or learning processes, teachers' and learners' attitudes, the implementation and evaluation of (the formal and the hidden) curricula, initial and in-service teacher training. No matter what focus is chosen, research methodology has to be collaborative, that is include all parties involved (teachers, policy makers, parents, learners, etc.), be grounded in the class and feedback into the class, emerge from the specific educational context but not miss out at the European level, and, finally, relate to more generalised improvement efforts in education.

References

Bausch, K.-R., Christ, H. and Krumm, H.-J. (eds.) (2003), *Handbuch Fremdsprachenunterricht. 4. Auflage* (Handbook of foreign language teaching, 4th edition), Tübingen, A. Francke Verlag.

Bausch, K.-R., Helbig-Reuter, B. in co-operation with Otten, E. and Schormann, R. (2003), "Überlegungen zu einem integrativen Mehrsprachigkeitskonzept: 14 Thesen zum schulischen Fremdsprachenlernen" (Thoughts on an integrative multilingualism concept: 14 theses on school foreign language learning), *Neusprachliche Mitteilungen*, 56 (4), 194-201.

Bebermeier, H. et al. (2003), "Fremdsprachliches Lehren und Lernen in der Primarstufe und in den Eingangsklassen der Sekundarstufe I: Positionspapier (Kurzfassung)" (Foreign language learning in primary education and at the beginning of secondary education I: theses (abridged version), *Neusprachliche Mitteilungen*, 56 (1), 2-4.

Blondin, C. et al. (1998), *Fremdsprachen für die Kinder Europas. Ergebnisse und Empfehlungen der Forschung* (Foreign languages for Europe's children. Research outcomes and advice), Berlin, Cornelsen Verlag.

Bludau, M. (1998), "Vom Abholen und vom Weiterführen" (On receiving and continuing), *Neusprachliche Mitteilungen*, 51 (3), 157-160.

Cameron, L. (2001), *Teaching languages to young learners. Cambridge Language Teaching Library*, Cambridge, Cambridge University Press.

Christ, H. (2003), "Erwerb von Fremdsprache im Vorschul- und Primarschulalter" (Foreign language acquisition in kindergarten and primary education), in Bausch, K.-R., Christ, H. and Krumm, H.-J. (eds.), *Handbuch Fremdsprachenunterricht. 4. Auflage* (Handbook of foreign language teaching. 4th edition), Tübingen, A. Francke Verlag, 449-454

Edelenbos, P. and Johnstone, R. (eds.) (1996), *Researching languages at primary school. Some European perspectives*, London, CiLT.

European Commission (2003), *Förderung des Sprachenlernens und der Sprachenvielfalt: Aktionsplan 2004-2006* (Promoting language learning and linguistic variation: Action plan 2004-2006), 449.

European Commission (2004), Directorate-General for Education and Culture, Lifelong learning: education and training policies. Multilingualism policies (2004), "Implementation of the education and training 2010 work programme. Working group 'Languages' progress report", December 2004, EXP LG/13/2004.

Gattullo, F. and Pallotti, G. (2003), "Baseline study on FLT to young learners in Italy", in Nikolov, M. and Curtain, H. (eds.), *An early start: young learners and modern languages in Europe and beyond*, Strasbourg, Council of Europe Publishing, 51-58.

Helfrich, H. (1999), "Fremdsprachenarbeit an Grundschulen und das Problem der Progression. Erfahrungen aus Rheinland-Pfalz" (Foreign language work in primary schools and the progression problem. Experience in Rheinland-Pfalz), *PRAXIS Fremdsprachenunterricht*, 1, 60-66.

Hurrell, A. and Satchwell, P. (eds.) (1996), *Reflections on modern languages in primary education. Six UK case studies*, London, CiLT.

Kubanek-German, A. (2001), *Kindgemäßer Fremdsprachenunterricht, Band 1: Ideengeschichte* (Children-appropriate foreign language teaching, Volume 1: concepts review), Münster, Waxmann Verlag.

Kubanek-German, A. (2003), *Kindgemäßer Fremdsprachenunterricht, Band 2: Didaktik der Gegenwart* (Children-appropriate foreign language teaching, Volume 2: current teaching methodology), Münster, Waxmann Verlag.

Low, L. and Wolfe, L. (1996), "MLPS: impact on the secondary sector", in Hurrell, A. and Satchwell, P. (eds.), *Reflections on modern languages in primary education. Six UK case studies*, London, CiLT, 29-38.

Mertens, J. (2001), "Der Fremdsprachenunterricht am Wendepunkt. Zum Verhältnis von Grundschule und Sekundarschule" (Foreign language teaching on the turning point. About the relationship between primary and secondary education), *Neusprachliche Mitteilungen*, 54 (4), 194-202.

Mindt, D. and Schlüter, N. (2003), *Englisch in den Klassen 3 und 4. Grundlagen für einen ergebnisorientierten Unterricht* (English in classes 3 and 4. Basis for outcome-oriented teaching), Berlin, Cornelsen Verlag.

Nikolov, M. and Curtain, H. (eds.) (2003), *An early start: young learners and modern languages in Europe and beyond*, Strasbourg, Council of Europe Publishing.

Piepho, H.-E. (2001), "Was müssen weiterführende Schulen vom Grundschulfremdsprachenunterricht erwarten dürfen?" (What are secondary schools entitled to expecting from foreign language teaching in primary education?), *PRAXIS Fremdsprachenunterricht*, 48 (4), 346-354.

Rück, H. (2004), "Prinzipien des frühen Fremdsprachenerwerbs" (Principles of early foreign language acquisition), *Neusprachliche Mitteilungen*, 57 (4), 198-207.

Sauer, H. (2000), "Frühes Fremdsprachenlernen in Grundschulen – Ein Irrweg?" (Early foreign language learning in primary education – In the wrong direction?), *Neusprachliche Mitteilungen*, 53 (1), 2-7.

Schmid-Schönbein, G. (2001), *Didaktik: Grundschulenglisch. Anglistik – Amerikanistik*" (Teaching methodology: English in primary education. English – American Studies), Berlin, Cornelsen Verlag.

Steinbrügge, L. (2003), "Neue Konzepte für den Fremdsprachenerwerb" (New concepts for foreign language acquisition), *Neusprachliche Mitteilungen*, 56 (1), 16-23.

About the author

Charis-Olga Papadopoulou is a lecturer of German as a Foreign Language Teaching Methodology at the Department of German Language and Literature, Aristotle

University of Thessaloniki. Her M.Sc. was on Educational Research Methodology (University of Oxford, UK) and her D.Phil. on Foreign Language Teacher Thinking (University of Oxford, UK). Her research interests relate to early foreign language learning, reflective teaching, alternative assessment methods, L3 acquisition and continuity in foreign language learning.

Chapter 8
Learners' own cultural identity in early language learning

Gloria Vickov

1.   Introduction

Foreign language teaching programmes in many European countries emphasise learners' ability to use a foreign language to talk about their homeland and its culture. This should lead to better cross-cultural understanding and to developing learners' awareness of their cultural identity. Primary English teachers in Croatia, however, often mention learners' difficulty in presenting their own culture and tradition in English, as learners are overwhelmed with information related to Anglo-Saxon culture. A possible cause for this may lie in current primary English coursebooks which expose young learners to mainly stereotyped target language cultural information.

Throughout the centuries, preserving and fostering cultural heritage and tradition have been of crucial importance to every nation in ensuring its survival and recognisable ethnic identity. This makes the cultural dimension not only a lifeline of national existence and continuity, but also the main source of differences between one's own national identity and otherness. It is no surprise, therefore, that many foreign language (FL) experts have realised the growing importance of incorporating cultural elements into FL teaching (Brewster and Ellis, 2003; Byram and Feng, 2002; Kramsch, 1996; Kubanek-German, 2000; Peck, 1984; Petravić, 2004; Ur, 1991; Vilke, 1991). According to Peck (1984), without the study of culture, FL instruction is inaccurate and incomplete. The teaching of a target culture provides FL learners with an opportunity to understand and respect the target culture native speakers, their tradition and way of life. This should lead to the development of intercultural awareness, which, as explained by Kubanek-German (2000, p. 50), stands for "the ability to see oneself as part of a larger community, to contrast cultures, to be aware that a different language is embodying different cultural beliefs, behaviours and meanings". Brewster and Ellis (2003) point out that in today's multicultural world, which faces globalisation within sophisticated communication technologies, an increasing number of countries, such as those within the European Union, include cultural and intercultural awareness as well as intercultural learning as part of their educational and language teaching policies to promote international understanding and world peace.

Recently, some authors (Petravić, 2004; Tas, 2005; Tsui, 2005; Vickov, 2005) have been advocating the idea of introducing the elements of FL learners' homeland culture into FL teaching. They see it primarily as a means to promote a deeper understanding of one's own culture, which seems to be a necessary prelude to better cross-cultural understanding and tolerance. A further benefit of incorporating FL learners' own cultural elements into FL teaching is related to possible pedagogical implications aimed at improving learners' communicative competence and raising the level of their aspiration and motivation. This seems to be particularly important in early FL learning because it is at an early age that FL learning is experienced on a positive note with children being highly motivated (Mihaljević-Djigunović, 1998; Vilke, 1991). Furthermore, it is at this age that children start to discover both their local and wider environment systematically, forming at the same time their first attitudes and knowledge about the world around them.

The focus of our study is on incorporating learners' own cultural identity into early FL teaching, with special attention to English as a foreign language (EFL). This issue will be discussed primarily on the basis of the Croatian EFL teaching programme as it lays emphasis on learners' ability to use English to talk about their homeland and its culture. Primary English teachers in Croatia, however, often mention learners' difficulty in presenting their own culture and tradition in English, as learners are overwhelmed with information related to Anglo-Saxon culture. A possible cause for this may lie in current primary English coursebooks which expose young learners to mainly stereotyped target language cultural information. Therefore, the present chapter provides an analysis of four English coursebooks currently used with young learners in Croatian primary schools. It is worth pointing out that four years ago, English was introduced into the Croatian national curriculum as an obligatory school subject from the first grade of primary school, that is, from the very start of formal schooling. This, we believe, additionally supports the idea of the Croatian EFL teaching programme being an adequate area for introducing young learners' own cultural values into early EFL.

2.   Background

As the intention of this paper is to provide an insight into the possibility of introducing elements of young learners' own cultural heritage and tradition into early foreign language learning, there is a need for clarification of the terms "culture" and "cultural identity" as they will be used in the paper. The term "culture" encompasses a wide range of elements related to one's nationhood, covering both formal and deep culture. Formal culture, as defined by Brooks (1983, cited in Peck, 1984, p. 210), includes art, music, literature, technology, architecture and politics, whereas deep culture refers to a particular nation's lifestyle: their eating habits, folk customs, what they do for a living, how they express their attitudes towards their friends and family members and the like. Similarly, Kramsch (1996) provides two definitions of the term "culture" denoting two ways of defining a social community. The first definition comes from the humanities and, like Brooks' formal culture, focuses on the way a social group represents itself and others through its material productions (works of art, literature, social institutions ...). The second definition comes from the social sciences referring to the attitudes and beliefs, ways of thinking and behaving shared by members of a community. This latter definition, which corresponds to Brooks' deep culture, constitutes what Peck (1984, p. 2) calls "a cushion between a man and his environment" and represents the most profitable way of looking at culture with regard to FL instruction. Peck justifies this statement by saying that if we provide our learners only with a list of historical or geographical facts and a list of lexical items, we have not provided them with an intimate view of real life in the target culture.

Discussing the issue of cultural identity, within a more general view on cultural perceptions of racial, ethnic and national identity, Kramsch defines it as "bureaucratically or self-ascribed membership in a specific culture" (1998, p. 126). In our study, the notion of cultural identity therefore covers the learners' membership in both their homeland's formal and deep culture. It also relates to the membership in all the spiritual and material values of their local environments.

The teaching of culture as a component of foreign language instruction has recently been stressed as a means of promoting international understanding and world peace. This domain of foreign language teaching currently operates within three approaches: cross-cultural, intercultural and multicultural. The nomenclature overlaps somewhat in its use. According to Kramsch, the term "cross-cultural" or "intercultural" usually refers to "the meeting of two cultures or two languages across the political boundaries of nation-states" (1998, p. 81). A cross-cultural approach seeks ways to understand the Other by learning his/her national language. The term "intercultural" may also refer to communication between people from different ethnic, social, gendered cultures within the boundaries of the same national language. Examples of these approaches can be found in the "intercultural communicative competence" advocated by Michael Byram and Anwei Feng (2002) or in attempts to create a culturally sensitive pedagogy on the basis of the impact of intercultural experiences on teacher professionalism (Gu, 2005). While the two approaches aim at developing an understanding of target cultures (within the framework of FL teaching), the multicultural approach refers to current initiatives in American FL education aimed at broadening and diversifying traditional views of culture beyond the boundaries of nation states. According to Mullen (1992, cited in Kramsch, 1996), multicultural education seeks to expand the traditional curriculum by incorporating issues of race, class and gender in order to sensitise students to the unique historical background of the United States culture.

One of the aspects of cross-cultural, intercultural or multicultural communication is the learner's ability to acquire another person's language and understand someone else's culture while retaining his/her own. Kramsch denotes this aspect as the concept of appropriation, "whereby learners make a foreign language and culture their own by adopting and adapting it to their own needs and interests" (1998, p. 81). This concept prompted us to draw a parallel between the above stated ability and the learner's ability to use a foreign language in order to promote his/her native culture and national identity. This seems to be highly important in the current process of accelerating globalisation in which many countries seek to promote their national and cultural identities as well in order to establish a good position on the world market. Regarding

EFL, there seems to be a consensus that in the process of globalisation, English has become a language of global communication, the lingua franca (ELF) and that learners do not primarily learn it in order to use it as a means of communication with native speakers. As recent research in Asia indicates, the functional significance of English in today's multicultural world is reflected not only in commercial and political issues, but also in making efforts to promote one's own national identity and to occupy a legitimate space in the process of globalisation (Tsui, 2005).

According to the *Common European Framework of Reference*, the majority of European countries also insist on developing and fostering their national identities, which is juxtaposed with other general objectives in FL learning, developing openness to foreign cultures being one of them. Their curricula also emphasise an interdisciplinary approach to teaching, within which FL teaching is seen as a means for acquiring and reinforcing the concepts of other school subjects as well (for example, in Finland).

A similar curriculum framework can be found in Croatia. In the domain of FL teaching, particularly English, the Croatian national curriculum places an emphasis on the common educational goal within which pupils should be trained to use a foreign language in order to talk about their local environment, their homeland, its natural resources and cultural values. This educational component of FL learning is aimed at the development and promotion of pupils' own national identity. It is believed that deeper understanding of one's own cultural identity is an essential prerequisite to intercultural learning, primarily in the sense of its impact on experiencing a target language culture. It was in 1991 that the Croatian national primary school curriculum introduced learners' own culture and civilisation into the FL teaching programme. The curriculum explicitly stated that learners should learn FL vocabulary items necessary for talking about their immediate environment and homeland (*National curriculum*, 1991, p. 59). This curriculum dimension is related to developing learners' own national identity, which is, in its general educational goal, aimed at developing intercultural awareness and better understanding of both the European and worldwide multicultural society. In other words, as pointed out by Petravić (2004), the legitimate position of learners' own cultural elements in FL teaching is based on the cognition that understanding a foreign culture develops through the prism of one's own culture, and that understanding one's own national identity is a necessary prerequisite to developing intercultural understanding.

Developing the awareness of learners' own cultural identity and nationhood, forming thus a basis for understanding a target culture and developing the ability to talk about their own cultural and natural heritage, thus promoting it in today's globalised world, is not the only advantage of incorporating learners' native culture into FL teaching, particularly early FL teaching. Discussing young EFL learners and the issue of vocabulary acquisition at an early age, Vilke (1991) is quite explicit about what words children should learn at the early stages of FL learning. According to her findings, children should be exposed to those words the content of which is already familiar to them in their mother tongue. Apart from familiar meaning and from having a clear concept of the word being learned, it is also very important that the words come from the children's own culture and from their local environment. Familiarity enables them to speak about daily routines, about something that is happening here and now. It also provides them with an opportunity to apply their vocabulary knowledge on a regular basis in the world which surrounds them, thus being in a position to practise what they were taught at school as well as to use a language in a creative way. Children do not experience language as a system of forms but as a means of expressing meaning. As Halliday (1973) once stated, they are not interested in what language is, but what can be done with it. Judging by Ville's research results, it is assumed that children simply transfer the concepts previously acquired in their mother tongue within their own culture into a foreign language giving these concepts new names.

When it comes to unknown concepts from a target language culture, the process appears to be much more complex: with their teacher's help they have to acquire both a new concept and memorise its name in a foreign language. An additional difficulty lies in the fact that their surrounding world does not provide verification of the correctness of their perception of a newly acquired concept. Croatian children, for example, do not experience the English word "kettle" by seeing one of their household members filling it with water and putting it onto a cooking stove. Similarly, being exposed to the sentence "Go upstairs to bed", a boy commented in Croatian that he also went "upstairs to bed", because he had a bunk bed and that his little brother slept on the lower bed and he slept on the upper one. Needless to say, these children should have been provided with an explanation regarding the system of a typical English house. If this is done in an interesting and appropriate way, children usually accept it. At the same time, they will become aware of other nations' customs and lifestyles. In this particular case, we see, however, no reason not to first introduce vocabulary items the content of which is present in the children's own environment – a bunk bed stands for a type of bed usually found in Croatian families with two or more children.

Experience with the words denoting foreign culture elements could be a very useful guideline to authors of early FL teaching materials. When thinking about what vocabulary items they should include in their coursebooks, we believe, two starting points should be taken into consideration. Firstly, at an early age, a foreign language usually presents a great challenge and thus a powerful motivational factor (Dunn, 1993). Secondly, children at this age start discovering in a systematic way all the things that surround them, which induces them to form their first perceptions of the values present both in their local and wider environment. It is in this positive attitude towards foreign languages at the initial stages of learning and a high degree of motivation and children's curiosity that we see the possibility of incorporating the elements of children's own cultural and traditional background into FL teaching. Associating linguistic and extralinguistic context in this direction is likely to result in a twofold advantage: on the one hand, children learn a foreign language, and on the other, they renew their existing knowledge of their cultural heritage receiving at the same time new information. In this way, they also develop their local and national identity. Apart from this, we expect that the application of the newly acquired vocabulary knowledge would be in this way considerably facilitated and prompted due to better availability of the extralinguistic context. This again brings young pupils closer to experiencing success, which would then, we assume, exert a considerable impact on their motivation. One of the aspects of experiencing success at an early age in the process of FL learning is reflected in a situation when a child uses a foreign language to talk about his/her everyday environment, which is usually followed by his/her parents' and other adults' warm approval (Vickov, 2005). Therefore, it is highly important for young learners to be provided, whenever possible, with an opportunity to use a foreign language in non-institutional surroundings. This would enable them to get a clear insight into the justifiability and practicality of all their efforts, it would ensure their experiencing success and it would enrich their knowledge of the cultural context.

3.   The study: an analysis of coursebooks

Although English has been introduced as a compulsory school subject from Year 1 of primary school, and although developing young learners' own cultural and national identity within an interdisciplinary approach from the earliest stages of primary schooling has been a component of the Croatian FL syllabus, primary English teachers in Croatia often mention learners' difficulty in presenting their own culture and tradition in English. They claim their pupils lack basic vocabulary when it comes to identifying their immediate cultural and traditional environment. They also regret not having an interdisciplinary parallel with other school subjects, primarily science, geography, history and Croatian (as mother tongue), in which the elements of the Croatian cultural background are taught on a regular basis. Such a situation could be, at least, partially justified by the fact that vocabulary items related to the Croatian cultural and traditional background are almost totally neglected in the English coursebooks currently used in Croatian primary schools.

In our study a quantitative analysis of the elements of Croatian cultural information was conducted in order to establish the extent of their representation. The analysis was made using a sample of four English coursebooks currently used in Croatian primary schools. The same procedure was followed with regard to the elements of the Anglo-Saxon culture. For this purpose, we chose the following coursebooks: *Dip in 3* (Mardešić, 2003, Year 3 coursebook), *Dip in 4* (Ban and Blažić, 2006, Year 4 coursebook), *Building bridges 5* (Lubina et al., 2006, Year 5 coursebook) and *Way to go 5* (Mardešić and Džeba, 2004, Year 8 coursebook). All coursebooks are publications of Croatian publishers. In the analysis, the focus of our interest was on those culturally coloured vocabulary items which appear in the coursebooks as part of a clear cultural context, either Croatian or Anglo-Saxon.

In the first part of the analysis, lexical items are individually identified in tabular form with regard to their cultural origin and the primary school year they refer to. The table is followed by a chart comparing the representation of the vocabulary items related to

Anglo-Saxon culture to the representation of the vocabulary items related to Croatian culture. Both the table and chart data provide a detailed account of the amount and type of culturally coloured items from both cultures and are expected to identify an overall view concerning the extent to which Croatian primary schoolchildren are exposed to Anglo-Saxon culture and Croatian culture, respectively.

4.   What coursebooks contain

Tables 1 and 2 present the vocabulary items identified in the four coursebooks denoting elements of Anglo-Saxon and Croatian culture respectively.

Table 1: Vocabulary items related to Anglo-Saxon and Croatian culture in EFL coursebooks (Years 3 and 4)

Year 3: *Dip in 3*		Year 4: *Dip in 4*	
Anglo-Saxon culture	**Croatian culture**	**Anglo-Saxon culture**	**Croatian culture**
A cowboy	the Adriatic Sea	a school uniform	Croatia
downstairs/upstairs	Croatia	upstairs/downstairs	Croatian
a study	Croatian	a dining room	
a double-decker	the River Sava	a skyscraper	
the Thames	the St Mark's Cathedral	pound	
the Guard Tower		the White House	
pound		the Statue of Liberty	
pence		the United States of America	
the London Eye		Disneyland	
London Bridge		cowboys	
the Queen		Indians	
Great Britain		a banjo	
Tower Bridge		Halloween	
Clock Tower		Hamburgers	
Regent's Park		baseball	
Buckingham palace		doughnuts	
St Paul's Cathedral		England	
Trafalgar Square			

Nelson's Column Oxford Street black taxis		Thanksgiving roast turkey pumpkin pie sweet potatoes McDonald's Native American story Harry Potter	

Table 2: *Vocabulary items related to Anglo-Saxon and Croatian culture in EFL coursebooks (Years 5 and 8)*

Year 5: Building bridges 5		Year 8: Way to go 5	
Anglo-Saxon culture	**Croatian culture**	**Anglo-Saxon culture**	**Croatian culture**
a blazer	Croatia	the Angles	Croatian
a school uniform	the Adriatic coast	the Saxons	Adriatic tours
brunch	Croatian	English settlers	
fish and chips	the Adriatic Sea	English Protestants	
the United Nations building	the Old Town	Oxford lecturer	
the Empire State Building	fortresses	Rugby school	
New Yorker	Palaces	British public schools	
the United Kingdom		British Empire	
the United States of America		Queen Victoria	
English		US Government organisation	
Harry Potter		Australia – Down Under	
Manchester United fan		the Aborigines	
Great Britain		Australians	
pounds		koala bears	
hamburgers		Australian wool	
England		Australian English	
		the Chicago Bulls	

the Indian		British Triathlon Association	
the Atlantic		Central America	
the Pacific		the Loch Ness Monster	
New York harbour		Central Park	
Statue of Liberty		Madison Square Garden	
skyscrapers		The New York Knicks	
Central Park		The Republic of Ireland	
dollars		Northern Ireland	
Brooklyn Bridge		black beer	
Halloween		St Patrick	
Easter egg role		Canadian	
Egg hunting		maple leaf	

The lists of items indicate a dominating presence of Anglo-Saxon cultural information covering various aspects of both formal and deep cultural background. The cultural areas presented by the lexical items referring to the target culture range from the historical dimension (for example, the Angles, the Saxons, English settlers, British Empire, Queen Victoria) mainly presented in the Year 8 coursebook to native speakers' eating habits (hamburgers, doughnuts, pumpkin pie, sweet potatoes). At the upper primary school level (Years 5 and 8) culturally related items are incorporated into topic-based units dealing with various aspects of the two cultures. For example, in the Year 5 coursebook *Building bridges 5*, apart from some other words, the following ones have been identified as vocabulary items related to Croatian culture: the Old Town, fortresses and palaces. These words are used in the coursebook for describing Dubrovnik, one of Croatia's most beautiful ancient towns, under the protection of UNESCO. Unlike other EFL coursebooks included in the study, *Building bridges 5* at least attempts to include, though vaguely, the learners' native culture and national identity by simply putting the main character, a Croatian girl named Ana, and her family as temporary emigrants (due to her parents' work) in Great Britain. It is through Ana that the learners are exposed to English lexical items related to Croatian culture. However, upon examination of the data presented in Table 2, one can easily come to the conclusion that even in this case the Croatian cultural background is only symbolically represented (there are only seven lexical items that explicitly refer to the learners' own national and cultural identity: Croatia, the Adriatic coast, Croatian, the Adriatic Sea, the Old Town, fortresses and palaces).

The most obvious discrepancy in the representation of the target and native cultural information occurs in the Year 8 coursebook in which all the cultural topic-based units deal exclusively with Anglo-Saxon concepts. The areas covered by target culture elements relate to sport (Rugby School, the Chicago Bulls, the British Triathlon Association and the New York Knicks), education (Oxford lecturer, British public schools and Australian English), historical, geographical and governmental issues (British Empire, Queen Victoria, the US Government, the Aborigines, Australians, Central America and the Republic of Ireland) as well as traditional and local environment elements (English Protestants, Australian wool, the Loch Ness Monster, black beer, St Patrick and maple leaf).

As to the lower classes of primary school (Years 3 and 4), the coursebooks do not deal with cultural topics. All the elements coming from Anglo-Saxon culture (see Table 1) are incorporated into units thematically in relation to the following topics: family and friends, toys, school and home time, places and animals, which, generally speaking, stand for the usual topic areas presented in current EFL coursebooks for young learners. As can be seen from Table 1, *Dip in 3* offers some more information on Great Britain and London, in particular, within a lesson on London; the only example of a lesson explicitly dedicated to target culture information.

In accordance with the data obtained from the analysis of coursebooks for the upper classes, coursebooks for Years 3 and 4 scarcely offer any information related to the learners' own cultural background. It is almost symptomatic that the only cultural points related to Croatian culture and presented in the above stated coursebooks refer to the name of the country (Croatia) and the geographical item of the Adriatic Sea.

The collected vocabulary data were subjected to further statistical analysis comparing the representation of items related to Anglo-Saxon culture to the representation of vocabulary items related to Croatian culture.

Figure 1: Representation of the vocabulary items related to Anglo-Saxon and Croatian culture

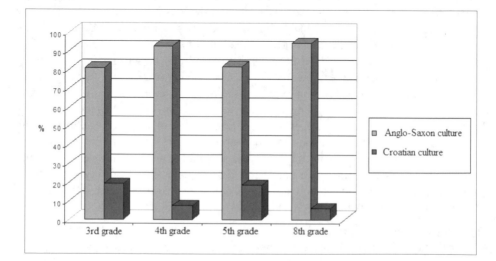

Judging by the results shown in the above chart, an obvious dominance of the target language cultural information has been confirmed as well as an almost complete absence of the elements related to Croatian cultural heritage. The vocabulary items related to the Anglo-Saxon culture account for between 80% and 93% of all the culturally coloured vocabulary items in the four coursebooks.

5.   Discussion

With no doubts whatsoever about the importance of exposing learners to information about the target culture to develop their intercultural awareness, as explained in the introduction, an almost total absence of the vocabulary area denoting the learners' own (Croatian) cultural background in the EFL coursebooks comes as a surprise, especially with regard to the theoretical postulates of the Croatian national curriculum. As has been shown, it lays an emphasis on the development of the learners' ability to use a foreign language, particularly English, for promoting their own national and cultural identity. This seems to be of crucial importance not only in the sense of preserving one's own cultural values and particularities in today's multicultural world, but also in the sense of establishing a legitimate place in the world's political and commercial arena. Learning about one's own cultural and national heritage appears to be vital for gaining a deeper understanding of self-identity and better cross-cultural understanding (Petravić, 2004).

The Croatian National Educational Standard (CNES), as one of the most recent educational initiatives in Croatia, puts a clear emphasis on preserving national and cultural identity. According to the CNES, school educational goals can be broken down into twenty categories including:

- care, preservation and promotion of cultural heritage as a part of national and cultural identity, as well as awareness of the values of cultural heritage within globalisation processes;

- promotion of love for and pride in homeland and country;

- recognition of one's own roots, recognition of and respect for other cultures and other civilisations' spiritual values (as a counterbalance to globalisation processes that might be perceived as a purely economic or technological reality).

Also, "educational materials and their interconnection with educational topics in various subjects … should support the development of the notion of national identity among pupils. Through learning about their roots and by developing a feeling of respect for their country, pupils will be able to define their own position in the world, to appreciate their own language and people while simultaneously appreciating and respecting the language of others" (CNES). A similar point related to introducing the

115

elements of the learners' own cultural identity into teaching materials can be found in the issue of intercultural representations discussed by Byram and Feng (2002). According to their research, some textbook writers are not enthusiastic about intercultural interpretations, as they fear that the learners may not be interested in them, particularly the texts about their own culture. The authors' work, however, suggests that this fear is not grounded. The same has been confirmed in a project of revising *Headway* as an EFL coursebook, undertaken by Tas (2005) at Baskent University in Turkey. Upon having identified the sections that were culturally loaded (for example, unfamiliar holidays like Halloween and Easter), Tas found texts like popular Turkish folk tales, local TV shows, commercials and celebrities juxtaposing them with their British counterparts. Exposure to interculturally coloured teaching materials empowered the learners by allowing them to produce texts about their own culture, to appreciate others' cultures and love what is genuinely Turkish.

Another reason for being surprised at the absence of the vocabulary area related to the learners' own (Croatian) cultural identity lies in the fact that introducing English as an obligatory school subject into Year 1 of primary school in Croatia was preceded by longitudinal research on early FL learning conducted by several prominent ELT methodology experts, Professor Vilke being one of them. As was explained earlier, Vilke as early as in 1991 emphasised the necessity of exposing young learners to the vocabulary items related to their own cultural and traditional background. The introduction of such an immediate extra-linguistic context into early EFL teaching enables young learners to apply their language knowledge on a regular basis in their immediate surrounding and, on the other hand, to foster and broaden their perceptions of their homeland and local cultural heritage. These postulates are incorporated also in a *Joint framework for assessing progress in teaching foreign languages and pupil self-evaluation*. According to the document, the competence in listening comprehension at the initial levels of A1 and A2 presupposes the learners' ability to recognise familiar words and very basic phrases concerning himself/herself, his/her family and immediate concrete surroundings/local area. Furthermore, with regard to the skills of writing and speaking, the stated levels presuppose the ability to write/speak also about areas of immediate needs, one's nationality, living conditions and the like.

6. Conclusions

Introducing the elements of young learners' own cultural heritage and tradition into early EFL learning is hoped to result in manifold advantages. Firstly, acquiring and reinforcing the knowledge of their home culture and tradition within an interdisciplinary parallel between EFL and other school subjects at an early school age could support developing young learners' own cultural and national identity, which seems to be a necessary prerequisite to better cross-cultural understanding. Secondly, providing young learners with the vocabulary items related to their homeland culture and tradition could serve, in the long run, as a basis for improving their communicative competence. According to the communicative approach, learners should be active, spontaneous and talkative while communicating in a foreign language (Kubanek-German, 2000). Such a demanding task could be facilitated, we believe, also by training young FL learners to use a foreign language to talk about themselves, about their local environment, their homeland and its cultural wealth and traditions. These categories are, as a rule, the elements which primary schoolchildren are supposed to be well acquainted with, and thus present a solid foundation for two-way communication. Thirdly, being able to use a foreign language, particularly English, to talk about one's own cultural and national identity is a step forward in promoting it and preserving it in the multicultural world of today. Further advantage of incorporating young learners' own cultural identity into early EFL is related to the "here-and-now" aspect of FL learning. According to this aspect, young EFL learners should be provided with the opportunity to speak about their daily routines, about something that is happening here and now (Vilke, 1991). This would enable them to use their newly acquired English vocabulary on a regular basis in their local environment. This again, we expect, would lead to a lot of opportunities for practising and creative uses of English as a foreign language.

References

Ban, S. and Blažić, D. (2006), *Dip in 4*, Year 4 English coursebook, Zagreb, Školska knjiga.

Brewster, J. and Ellis, G. (2003), *The primary English teacher's guide*, Penguin and Pearson Ed. Limited.

Brooks, N. (1983), "Teaching culture in the foreign language classroom", *Foreign Language Annals*, 16, New York, ACTFL.

Dunn, O. (1993), *Developing English with young learners*, London, Macmillan Publishers Ltd.

Feng, A. and Byram, M. (2002), "Authenticity in college English textbooks – An intercultural perspective", *RELC Journal,* 33 (2), 58-84.

Gu, Q. (2005), "Intercultural experience and teacher professional development", *RELC Journal,* 36 (1), 6-22.

Halliday, M. (1973), *Exploration in the functions of language*, London, Edward Arnold.

Kramsch, C. (1996), "The cultural component of language teaching", *Zeitschrift für Interkulturellen Fremdesprachenunterricht*, retrieved on 10 May 2007 from www.spz.tu_darmstadt.de/projekt_ejournal/jg-01-2/beitrag/kramsch2.htm.

Kramsch, C. (1998), *Language and culture*, Oxford, Oxford University Press.

Kubanek-German, A. (2000), "Emerging intercultural awareness in a young learner context: a checklist for research", in Moon, J. and Nikolov, M. (eds.), *Research into teaching English to young learners*, Pécs, University Press Pécs, 49-65.

Lubina, B.L., Neuhold, G., Pavuna, J. and Singer, D. (2006), *Building bridges 5*, Year 5 English coursebook, Zagreb, Profil.

Mardešić, M. (2003), *Dip in 3*, Year 3 English coursebook, Zagreb, Školska knjiga.

Mardešić, M. and Džeba, B. (2006), *Way to go 5*, Year 8 English coursebook, Zagreb, Školska knjiga.

Ministry of Science, Education and Sports (1991), *National curriculum*, Zagreb, Republic of Croatia.

Ministry of Science, Education and Sports (2004), *Primary school Croatian national educational standard*, available online at: www.mzos.hr.

Mihaljević-Djigunović, J. (1998), *The role of affective factors in foreign language learning*, Zagreb, Faculty of Philosophy, University of Zagreb.

Peck, D. (1984), "Teaching culture: beyond language", Yale-New Haven Teachers Institute. Retrieved on 9 May 2006 from www.yale.edu/ynhti/curriculum/units/1984/3/84.03.06.x.html.

Petravić, A. (2004), "Perception of foreign and native culture in German course books" (unpublished doctoral dissertation), Zagreb, Faculty of Philosophy, University of Zagreb.

Tas, E.I. (2005), "Exploiting students' own culture in EFL reading materials". Retrieved on 8 March 2007 from www.teachingenglish.org.uk/iatefl2005/ron_6_conf.shtml.

Tsui, A. (2005), "Language and identity". Retrieved on 11 February 2007 from www.teachingenglish.org.uk/iatefl2005/ron_6_conf.shtml.

Ur, P. (1991), *A course in language teaching*, Cambridge, Cambridge University Press.

Vickov, G. (2005), "Native cultural heritage and tradition as a non-linguistic context in early FL learning", in Ivon, H. (ed.), *From heritage to heritage, the cultural aspect of pre-school education*, Split, Teachers' Training College, 81-91.

Vilke, M. (1991), *Your child and language*, Zagreb, Školska knjiga.

About the author

Gloria Vickov is EFL lecturer at the Teachers' Training Department at the Faculty of Philosophy, University of Split. She has published a number of articles on early FL learning and on developing writing skills at an early age. Her current doctoral research at the University of Zagreb focuses on corpus linguistics and discourse analysis.

Chapter 9
English phonetics and phonology in the curriculum

Zeljka Zanchi

1.   Introduction

English phonetics and phonology have not been systematically and consistently included in primary and secondary school English teaching curricula. This seems to be creating major problems for students, future teachers of English, as it impedes their successful mastery of English phonology essential to any teacher of English as a foreign language (FL) to young learners. This chapter attempts to investigate the current situation in Croatian primary schools regarding the extent to which English phonology and especially phonemic transcription already exist in the curriculum, as well as how and at what age they are introduced. I questioned students at the end of primary school, their teachers, as well as students at the Teacher Training Department of the Faculty of Philosophy, University of Split. The results are presented and discussed in this chapter.

In order to improve the teaching of English to young learners, the curriculum should be redefined. It should include consistent and systematic work on phonetic and phonological aspects of the language, laying much more emphasis upon correct pronunciation and introducing phonemic transcription, preferably at an early age. Apart from grammar and vocabulary, the mastery of which undoubtedly contributes towards achieving proficiency in a foreign language, good pronunciation, a sense of rhythm and appropriate intonation are necessary prerequisites for clear and fluent speech, thereby creating a basis for successful communication.

However, this aspect has often been neglected, underrated or somehow taken for granted, in the belief that it will eventually spontaneously develop alongside other language skills with practice, frequent repetition and imitation of exemplary models (teachers, native speakers, the media, etc.). This may be true of the majority of European languages (French, German, Italian or Spanish). "In most languages there is a fairly clear correspondence between sounds and symbols: certain letters or combinations of letters are pronounced in certain ways, and if there are variations, these are governed by consistent rules" (Ur, 2004, p. 56). English, however, may be taken as an example of a language where this correspondence is missing. There are many exceptions, as well as numerous examples of "words whose pronunciation could not be logically predicted from their spelling and vice versa" (ibid., p. 56). In other words, the spelling significantly differs from pronunciation, preventing learners from using analogies in learning new words (for example, compare the pronunciation of "predict" and "indict", not to mention the generally known exceptional pronunciations of the grapheme "oo" in words such as "flood", "food", "foot" or "brooch"). This means that there are definitely no applicable generalisations: each new word has to be separately learnt, both its spelling and pronunciation. This is where the use of a good dictionary, providing reliable phonemic transcription, becomes imperative. However, the ability to read and understand the transcription requires certain basic knowledge of phonemic symbols and this is where the problem arises. Learners of English, regardless of their age and level, cannot do it on their own, neither can they be expected to unless given at least some instruction in basic phonology.

While rhythm and intonation may be spontaneously acquired through well-devised exercises and by imitating exemplary models, the latter is usually addressed through some other segments of teaching (namely, syntax or differentiation between statements, commands and questions, particularly the intonation of "yes"/"no" and "wh-" questions), the sounds of English, more precisely the phonemes, are rarely given the attention they undoubtedly deserve, especially if they are unfamiliar, that is do not exist in or considerably differ from the learners' mother tongue. This is where some basics of the English phonological system, most apparent in phonemic transcription, become a powerful tool towards achieving the goal.

Opinions have always been divided as to whether phonological issues should be deliberately and specifically taught or whether they should be included in the curriculum at all. This question has been addressed and formulated by Penny Ur (2004, p. 55), "Does pronunciation need to be deliberately taught? Won't it just be 'picked up'? If it does need to be deliberately taught, then should this be in the shape of specific pronunciation exercises, or casually, in the course of other oral activities?"

Experience has indeed shown that many learners, especially young ones, succeed in acquiring good pronunciation, especially stress, rhythm and intonation, by intuitive imitation. On the other hand, there is evidence that deliberate teaching of pronunciation does improve it, while consistent and systematic work on it is bound to result not only in better pronunciation, but also in an awareness of this segment of the language, as well as the ability to fully and competently use dictionaries in acquiring new vocabulary. This is especially true at university level: students of English are and should be expected to possess an adequate knowledge of all segments of the language, phonology by no means being the least important.

Working as a lecturer and language instructor at the Faculty of Philosophy in Split and teaching a number of courses, such as children's literature, Anglo-Saxon world, introduction to English grammar, language exercises and, last but not least, exercises in pronunciation, I have become increasingly aware of an urgent need to raise the overall level of teaching in preparing the future teachers of English to young learners (7-11 years of age), as well as concentrating on what I feel to be the most important issues.

2.   The problem

I have been teaching English majors for six years and I could not help noticing that the English phonological system seems to be creating serious problems for our students. In fact, it seems to be one of the most difficult courses. This may be due to a number of reasons. First, many students start their studies insufficiently prepared, believing a fair fluency in English and a good command of grammar and syntax, combined with the subsequent instruction in the methodology of teaching, to be the only skills required. While this is by all means true, at least to a certain extent, there are some aspects of learning and teaching a FL which are by no means less important. Unfortunately, when it comes to pronunciation, the importance of which cannot be overemphasised, particularly in teaching young learners, a great majority of students lack basic knowledge. Instead, they seem to rely exclusively on intuition, improvisation and playing by ear, which is both insufficient and unacceptable. Many students do not seem to realise the importance of exemplary pronunciation and the ability to pass it on to their pupils, thereby creating a basis for a future proficiency in English, which should be the ultimate goal of teaching a FL, especially at a university educating future teachers of the language.

This primarily results from the fact that English phonology is sadly neglected in our primary and secondary school English curricula. It is, if taught at all, less than adequately represented, with no consistency and no clear strategy. Teachers who consistently and systematically include the phonological aspect in their teaching curriculum, especially from the earliest age, are exceptionally rare. The consequences become obvious, which is best illustrated by the fact that the majority encounter the very notion and the basic facts of phonetics and phonology, such as distinguishing between different sounds of English, both vowels and consonants, especially when they are contrasted as distinct phonemes in minimal pairs and phonemic transcription, for the first time when they start attending the university course "Exercises in pronunciation of English". Not only are they unable to correctly pronounce or transcribe certain phonemes, but they are unable to recognise and discriminate them as linguistic segments affecting the meaning and frequently leading to misunderstanding and failing to convey the message, thus impeding effective communication. This may further result in students not being aware of the distinction between spelling and pronunciation, leading to insecurity and incompetence. Needless to say, those who are not fully aware of what they are saying and, even more importantly, how they are saying it can hardly be expected to become competent and efficient teachers of English. Apart from an exemplary pronunciation, which is, unarguably, a necessary prerequisite, a *condicio sine qua non* and which may, up to this point, have been spontaneously acquired, the students of English must be made extremely sensitive to this aspect of the language. They must possess the ability to rationally analyse and scrutinise their own speech if they are to teach others, which implies noticing errors, correcting them in the best possible way, and preventing their recurrence in the future. It is clear that it takes much more than simply being fluent in English to become a good teacher.

The situation is further exacerbated by some students' lack of motivation, stemming from the belief that English phonology does not need to be meticulously taught or learnt in primary school, that they themselves did not receive education on the subject, and that no one can expect them to teach what they themselves have never been taught. Furthermore, a number of students tend to approach the matter somewhat reluctantly, possibly discouraged by the prospect of having to learn a whole new set of signs and symbols represented by the phonemic transcription. Not everyone will encounter an equal degree of difficulty in the process: some students will naturally take longer to assimilate the basic knowledge and skills where phonology is concerned. Despite individual differences, they should all be encouraged to dedicate more time and effort to learning what will one day undoubtedly prove to be an enormous asset.

It is at this point that the lecturer encounters a series of problems which need to be immediately addressed and dealt with if they are to be quickly and efficiently resolved. Firstly, how to get the point across to the students, namely that mastering the basics of phonology is well worth the effort? How to make them see and realise the importance of what we are trying to teach them? Secondly, how to teach something that normally takes years in a relatively short time: one forty-five-minute period per week in three terms allotted to the course in the second and third years of study is obviously a rather demanding task.

3.   The study

These reasons led me to find out more about these issues, concentrating on pupils of upper grades of primary school (Years 7 and 8) and their teachers of English, with a view to analysing the current situation with respect to the teaching of pronunciation of English and corroborating, if possible, my initial hypothesis about English phonology not being sufficiently present in the curriculum.

It is with this aim in mind that I prepared three questionnaires: one for primary school pupils (114 participants), one for their teachers (four participants) and, finally, one for my third year students at the Faculty of Philosophy (43 participants). The idea of including this third set of questions occurred to me later, when the research was already in progress, as an additional means of shedding more light on the whole issue. Teaching English phonology in primary school and at university are certainly two entirely different things, both in their contents and methodological approaches. However, they may be perceived as closely connected. Whatever is taught (or not taught) in the early stages of learning a FL inevitably affects the learners' competence at more advanced levels. In other words, students of English who have not been taught the basics of phonology through their own school education are not adequately equipped to cope with it at the university level and consequently, as teachers, they are bound to neglect this aspect of teaching English. And this is where the circle closes.

My aim is to present the current situation and to examine negative attitudes which have so far prevented those responsible for creating a curriculum from seeing the overall picture and becoming aware of needs. Also, I would like to propose possible and feasible solutions to the problem.

4.   Analysis of teachers', pupils' and students' answers

4.1   The views of primary school teachers of English

Four primary school teachers of English were involved and asked the following questions. Their answers will be discussed right after the questions.

1. Are phonetics and phonology of the English language (the basics of the phonological system, phonemic transcription, teaching correct pronunciation, etc.) included in the primary English curriculum?

    (a) yes (1)

    (b) no (3)

The fact that three teachers gave a negative answer to this question shows that the phonological issues are absent from the curriculum. It is up to the teachers to decide when, at what level and in what way these items should be introduced, or whether they should be dealt with at all. Nevertheless, as will be seen in their answers to the subsequent question, it does not prevent some teachers from dedicating at least some of the available time to these, in my opinion, important issues.

2. If they are, do you think they are represented?

    (a) sufficiently (0)

    (b) insufficiently (4)

The answers to this question further show that teachers think English phonology is insufficiently present, although this point is not completely clarified and it may be arguable what is exactly meant by "sufficient representation".

3. Do the textbooks (students' books) you use provide phonemic transcription in their glossaries?
    (a) yes (4)

    (b) no (0)

The fact that coursebooks provide phonemic transcription raises the question of what purpose is supposed to be served if pupils, knowing nothing or very little about phonology, are not able to benefit from it by looking up new words and phrases and finding out how unfamiliar items are pronounced.

4. Which of the following do you do while presenting new texts, vocabulary items, etc.:

    (a) you pronounce particular vocabulary items (words, phrases) asking your pupils to repeat them after you, individually and/or in groups (1)

    (b) each new word is clearly written on the board and accompanied by phonemic transcription with an explanation of particular phonemic symbols, stress marks, etc. (0)

    (c) you do not have a systematic approach: it all depends on the level of difficulty or specific, possibly irregular, pronunciation of a particular word (3)

This may be taken as evidence of my initial claim about English phonology not being dealt with systematically and consistently, but rather at random, which is clearly insufficient to result in any knowledge.

5. How often do you introduce and explain to your pupils the pronunciation of particular phonemes and words, accompanying it with the correct phonemic transcription?

    (a) regularly and systematically (0)

    (b) occasionally, depending on the need (4)

    (c) not at all, as pupils will eventually acquire it by repeating and practising (0)

While none of the teachers dismisses the teaching of pronunciation as unnecessary, they obviously do not deal with it on a regular basis, which can hardly be expected to produce any lasting results.

6. If you do not systematically and methodically work on correct pronunciation, what are the reasons?

    (a) oversized classes (30 pupils or more) (4)

    (b) tight schedule (two or fewer lessons per week) is insufficient for more systematic work (4)

    (c) you think that primary school pupils would not be able to cope with it because English phonology is too difficult and therefore unsuitable for their age (0)

    (d) you simply do not consider it necessary because it would create additional (unnecessary) difficulties and would only be a waste of time (0)

Unanimous agreement in answering this question partly explains the reason why I believe phonology should be given more time. While all of the above is doubtless true (oversized classes and tight schedule), we cannot blame it for every setback or omission, certainly not for negligence. Again, if phonology should be given the appropriate time and space in the curriculum, that is if it were officially included in it, teachers would consequently feel obliged to deal with it much more regularly and systematically, in spite of undeniable difficulties.

7.   Do you think that English phonology should be included in the new curriculum?

(a) systematically and consistently, acquainting young learners with the English phonological system at an early school age (preferably in Years 3 or 4) (1)

(b) occasionally, as the need arises, but not before the upper years of primary school (Years 6, 7 or 8) (3)

(c) you do not consider it necessary in the early English classroom because pupils are bound to learn it in their own good time, in secondary school or later, especially if they intend to study the language more seriously (0)

While only one teacher thinks that the right age to start teaching pronunciation is the lower primary years, three agree that it should be done at a later time. They will probably argue that upper primary pupils are more mature, and therefore more capable of understanding new, abstract and sometimes complicated concepts. I would be inclined to agree with this, provided it is done on a regular and permanent basis. However, my experience in teaching young learners has shown that they can be successfully taught phonology on condition that it is introduced carefully and gradually, in a way well suited to that age.

It is not entirely surprising that the answers to particular questions seem to be, more or less, close to what I expected. For example, all four teachers feel the teaching of pronunciation and phonology to be insufficiently present in the primary school English curriculum. They also admit that they do not have a systematic approach to the problem and deal with phonological issues only occasionally. All agree that it is important, mentioning, however, objective difficulties as reasons for not being able to work on phonological issues more thoroughly and consistently. Most importantly, all four agree that teaching correct pronunciation (including the basics of phonology) should be given more attention and should definitely be part of the curriculum.

4.2   The views of primary school pupils

A total of 114 pupils from Years 7 and 8 filled in the questionnaire. The questions and answers are discussed below:

1.   *What do you find most difficult in learning English?*

(a) texts which include new words and expressions, their meaning, use, etc. (22 pupils = 19%)

(b) grammar (61 pupils = 54%)

(c) orthography (spelling), especially in view of the fact that there is a great difference between writing and pronunciation in the English language (31 pupils = 27%)

The answers to this question should not be surprising: English grammar has been traditionally regarded as a problem area by most learners, regardless of age or level. What is somewhat unexpected, however, is that as many as 31 pupils (27%) should view spelling as difficult, the reasons for which can be easily explained. This corroborates my opinion that spelling and pronunciation should be dealt with simultaneously, making the young learners aware of frequent dichotomies between the two, drawing their attention to some regularities, as well as to exceptions, and training them to identify both the phonemes and the graphemes, particularly the ones that are easily confused. This should be carefully done, taking into consideration the pupils' age and applying suitable methods and approaches.

2. *Have you learnt and practised phonemic transcription (a special alphabet used for writing down pronunciation)?*

(a) yes (13 pupils – 2 in private foreign languages schools = 11%)

(b) a little (49 pupils = 43%)

(c) no (52 pupils = 46%)

It is symptomatic that only 11% of respondents have learnt some basics of phonology, while many have little (43%) or no knowledge at all (46%), which together makes up 101 pupils or 89%, an exceptionally high percentage. This might be taken as a warning, indicating that more time should indeed be set apart for dealing with this important issue.

3. *Are you familiar with the symbols of the phonemic alphabet, namely those signs which serve to write down the pronunciation?*

(a) yes (12 pupils = 11%)

(b) a little, only some of them (61 pupils = 54%)

(c) no (41 pupils = 36%)

4. *Are you able to learn the pronunciation of new words on your own, by looking them up in a dictionary and referring to the special letters (symbols) written in brackets?*

(a) yes (31 pupils = 27%)

(b) partly (54 pupils = 47%)

(c) no (29 pupils = 25%)

The answers to questions 3 and 4 show an obvious inconsistency, especially compared to the ones given to question 2: they are actually in contradiction. While only 12 pupils (11%) claim that they are fairly familiar with phonemic symbols, as many as 31 pupils (27%) say that they are able to recognise and read the phonemic transcription from a dictionary. It strikes me as highly improbable. This may have resulted from some pupils not fully understanding the question(s). Again, the number of those whose answer is negative amounts to 41 (36%), which is by no means negligible. It would seem that this also goes to prove my initial hypothesis that phonology is indeed an area which definitely requires attention, certainly more than it has received so far.

5. *How do you learn the correct pronunciation of particular words and phrases?*

  (a) by copying from the board the pronunciation in the brackets written in phonemic symbols (2 pupils = 2%)

  (b) by using a dictionary giving correct pronunciation (38 pupils = 60%)

  (c) exclusively "by ear'", trying to imitate others' pronunciation (teacher, film, TV, etc.) (74 pupils = 65%)

This is another bit of evidence in accordance with my expectations. Again, the number of pupils claiming to be able to use a dictionary in learning the pronunciation of unfamiliar words is unrealistically high (38 pupils or 60%), whereas the vast majority (74 pupils or 65%) learn pronunciation "by ear", which, given the amount of time dedicated to a systematic teaching of pronunciation, was to be expected.

6. *Do you think that knowing phonemic symbols (phonemic transcription) would help you in learning pronunciation and make it easier for you?*

  (a) yes (57 pupils = 50%)

  (b) I do not know/I am not sure (33 pupils = 29%)

  (c) no (24 pupils = 21%)

Apart from the fact that the number of pupils who do not think they would benefit from being systematically taught phonology or are not quite sure about it (answers under b and c, respectively) amounts to 57 (50%), exactly the same number believe that it would be useful and would welcome a more consistent approach to it. I find this rather encouraging, particularly from the point of view of motivation. In my opinion, it should make those responsible for creating the English curriculum at least give it some thought.

As may have been expected, most pupils find grammar the most difficult aspect of learning English; however, the number of those who mention English spelling and pronunciation as a problematic area cannot be neglected. A majority of primary school pupils (101 or 89%) have received very little or no instruction on these particular issues, which further proves my point, corroborating my initial hypothesis about pronunciation being neglected and insufficiently included in the curriculum.

129

4.3   University students' views

Some 43 third year students were involved and answered the following questions.

1. *Which of the following do you find the most difficult?*

    (a) texts which include new vocabulary, phrases and idioms, their meaning, collocations and usage (7 students = 16%)

    (b) grammar (16 students = 37%)

    (c) writing, particularly orthography (spelling) (2 students = 5%)

    (d) phonetics and phonology (the material covered by the course "Exercises in English Pronunciation") (18 students = 42%)

As is the case with primary school pupils, a significant number of students seem to encounter difficulties in English grammar; however, rather surprisingly, there is an almost equal number of respondents who consider phonology as a particularly problematic area. This, of course, as will be pointed out later, is largely due to the fact that this aspect of English was hardly present in their primary and secondary education.

2. *When did you first meet the basics of phonology, the English phonological system, and the phonemic alphabet and transcription?*

    (a) in the lower years of primary school (4 students = 9%)

    (b) in the upper years of primary school (4 students = 9%)

    (c) in secondary school (6 students= 14%)

    (d) at university (29 students = 67%)

The percentage of students (67%) who had not learnt anything at all as far as English phonology is concerned before they started university is, in my opinion, alarmingly high. As expected, the area was given somewhat more attention in secondary education, although far from sufficient.

3. *Did your primary and secondary school teachers of English teach correct pronunciation, English phonology, transcription, etc.?*

    (a) regularly and systematically (1 student = 2%)

    (b) occasionally, if they considered it necessary (16 students = 37%)

    (c) never (hardly ever at all) (26 students = 61%)

This again shows that there are indeed few primary and secondary teachers of English who seriously deal with the matters of pronunciation and phonology. While it may prove of little or no consequence to the students who will use English merely as a means of communication, those who have chosen to pursue teaching the language as a career are bound to find it a gross disadvantage, as will be exemplified by the students' answers to the following question.

4. *Do you consider yourself deprived in this respect, that is, as a future teacher of English, do you think of it as a disadvantage?*

    (a) yes, if we had been thoroughly and systematically taught, we would now find it much easier (26 students = 61%)

    (b) it would be good if we had more knowledge, but I think it can always be learnt (13 students = 30%)

    (c) no, I do not consider it very important (4 students = 9%)

There is a remarkably large number of students (91%) whose answers (a and b respectively) clearly show that they are fully aware of the importance of phonological issues and indeed consider themselves deprived because they did not receive adequate instruction during their primary and secondary education. I believe that this figure alone should suffice to make those responsible for designing and implementing the English curriculum to at least think twice before they possibly decide to dismiss the issue as inconsequential.

5. *Do you think that the basics of English phonetics and phonology should be included in the curriculum?*

    (a) yes (30 students = 70%)

    (b) the decision should be left to primary school teachers and their own judgment (10 students = 23%)

    (c) no, I do not consider it necessary (3 students = 7%)

Here the number of answers under a and b (those who say "yes" together with those who seem to have some reservations concerning the issue) amounts to 93%, which again proves that introducing phonology and making it an integral part of both the primary and secondary English curricula should be given serious consideration, to say the very least.

6. *Do you think that English phonetics and phonology should be taught?*

    (a) systematically and consistently, preferably in the lower primary years (for example, Year 3) (11 students = 26%)

    (a) occasionally, according to the need, but not before the upper years (6, 7 or 8) (23 students = 54%)

    (c) perhaps later, but not before secondary school, concentrating on those pupils who wish to deal with the language more thoroughly and studiously (9 students = 21%)

As is the case with methodologists and practising teachers, the opinions are similarly divided. Not everyone agrees on the most suitable time, that is, age and level of learning, when phonology should be introduced. However, all respondents agree about the necessity to teach it, which means that they are, at least to a certain extent, aware of its importance. This again creates some ground for optimism, however moderate.

Finally, the students' answers clearly show that similar problems crop up at the university level as well, the numbers of those who find grammar and phonology the most difficult and problematic area are almost equal. A minority of students received some instruction in pronunciation in their primary and secondary school education, while the rest, the majority, encountered it for the first time at the faculty, in their second year of study. Consequently, they think that a good knowledge in this area would be beneficial, which is one more reason why it should be included in the curriculum. However, they seem to disagree on when or at what level it should be done. Most participants seem to consider the upper years of primary school (approximately between the ages of 11 and 14) to be the optimum time.

Conclusion

There has been a lot of dispute and disagreement among experts on the methodology of teaching English, as well as among primary and secondary school teachers, not only as to the relevance of teaching the basics of phonology, but also as to when it should be taught. This particularly applies to teaching phonemic transcription. Many teachers seem to be reluctant to do it, some of them rejecting the very idea as being highly impracticable or even useless, therefore no more than a waste of time. One cannot help thinking that the reasons may sometimes lie in some teachers' own incompetence to efficiently cope with the task (Bobda, 2006), due to the fact that they have themselves been inadequately prepared.

Far from claiming that good acquisition and, consequently, proficiency in English directly (or indirectly, for that matter) depends upon phonemic transcription, I still maintain that, properly taught, it helps to make learners of any age more sensitive to this aspect of learning a foreign language, especially one as irregular and as difficult in this respect as English. The basics of the English phonological system, phonemic transcription being only one of its many segments, contributes towards raising learners' awareness of this important but, unfortunately, long neglected aspect. Furthermore, it enables learners to make full use of dictionaries: without being familiar with phonemic transcription this is rendered impossible. Last, but not least, it is essential to all those learners intending to study English more thoroughly and seriously, particularly those preparing for a career in teaching. Teachers of English, apart from having an exemplary pronunciation, are expected to be able to competently pass it on to learners, teaching them how certain phonemes, words and sentences are pronounced, explaining to them the underlying basic rules, making them aware of the appropriate rhythm and intonation, drawing their attention to the phonemes of English which do not exist in, or significantly depart from those of, their mother tongue. This is precisely why I believe good training in the basics of phonology, with an emphasis upon practical issues, is invaluable and indeed becomes imperative.

Based on the results of this research, I propose that the basics of English phonology (including phonemic transcription) be introduced as early as possible since it is precisely at this age that the learners most promptly and easily acquire almost all aspects of the language, particularly pronunciation. I consider it to be too important to be left to mere chance or individual initiative.

Having taught English at the Foreign Languages Centre in Split for fifteen years, almost exclusively to young learners (mainly between the ages of 5 and 12), I have obtained a certain experience with this particular age group. I started introducing phonemic transcription, of course gradually but nevertheless regularly and consistently, to 9 and 10 year olds without any problems. I dedicated a part of each lesson (no more than five or ten minutes at the most) to introducing phonemic symbols as part of a game, allowing the children to get used to them. Not only did they learn transcription amazingly well, they also seemed to enjoy it immensely and I sincerely hope that it helped them at more advanced stages of learning.

Finally, I would like to quote Professor Mirjana Vilke-Prebeg (1991), an outstanding Croatian expert in English teaching methodology, a pioneer of early language learning. She says that the long-maintained opinion according to which children need not be deliberately or specifically taught pronunciation, because they would eventually learn it on their own, only applies to a second language (in the case of bilingualism), but not to a foreign language. Children do need professional help, even in learning pronunciation, because their exposure to the foreign language (two lessons per week at most) is far from sufficient for it to be spontaneously acquired. Phonology is clearly not an end in itself, but it is certainly a vital segment of any language, closely related to and intertwined with grammar, syntax, lexicology and semantics. It is also for this reason that it should be included in the English teaching curriculum, preferably at an early age, and developed simultaneously and harmoniously with other language skills.

Acknowledgements

I would like to express my most sincere gratitude to Ljiljana Jaman, Silvana Grmoja, Nina Koceic and Sandra Saric, teachers of English in Osnovna skola Lucac in Split and their pupils, as well as to my students at the Faculty of Philosophy, University of Split, without whose generous help and co-operation this paper would have been impossible.

References

Bobda, A.S. (2006), "Testing pronunciation", *English Teaching Forum*, 33.

Griffiths, B. (no year), "Integrating pronunciation into classroom activities". Retrieved from www.teachingenglish.org on 3 Mach 2006.

Ur, P. (2004), *A course in language teaching*, Cambridge, Cambridge University Press.

Vilke-Prebeg, M. (1991), *Vase dijete i jezik* (Your child and the language), Zagreb, Školska knjiga.

About the author

Zeljka Zanchi is a lecturer and language instructor at the Faculty of Philosophy, University of Split, Croatia. She graduated from the Faculty of Philosophy, University of Zagreb, in English Language and Literature and Comparative Literature. She has worked as a primary and secondary teacher of English, as well as in the Foreign Languages Centre in Split, teaching elementary, intermediate, advanced and proficiency courses, and has also worked as a translator and interpreter.

Chapter 10
Motivation pour l'apprentissage d'une langue étrangère dans deux régions frontalières (Espagne-France) pour des élèves de 8-12 ans

Luisa Pellicer

Abstract

The aim of the project presented in this chapter was to find schools in the neighbouring French region and establish correspondence between French and Spanish pupils. The goal was to create an opportunity for Spanish pupils to exchange letters with pen pals from France over a period of a school year, at the end of which there would be an exchange programme of pupils. Spanish pupils would travel to France and French pupils to Spain so that pupils from the two countries would have the opportunity to use the target language (either French or Spanish) in authentic situations. The chapter presents and describes the correspondence project between French and Spanish pupils. It also suggests ways of using correspondence between schools in different countries in order to enhance young language learners' language skills, motivation and cultural awareness.

Résumé

Le projet présenté dans ce chapitre avait pour but de trouver des écoles dans les régions françaises voisines afin de mettre en place une correspondance entre élèves espagnols et français. L'objectif était de donner aux élèves espagnols l'opportunité de faire un échange par lettres avec des correspondants français pendant toute une année scolaire, avec une visite d'échange des élèves à la fin de celle-ci. Il était prévu que les élèves espagnols aillent en France et vice-versa afin que les apprenants des deux pays aient l'occasion d'utiliser la langue cible (l'espagnol ou le français) dans des situations authentiques. Le chapitre présente et décrit le projet de correspondance entre les élèves espagnols et français. Il fait également des suggestions sur comment utiliser la correspondance entre des écoles dans différents pays afin d'améliorer les compétences linguistiques des jeunes apprenants de langues, leur motivation et leur éveil culturel.

1.   Introduction

Nous traitons ici de la motivation des jeunes apprenants de langues étrangères dans deux régions frontalières: la région du nord de l'Aragon en Espagne et la région du sud de l'Aquitaine en France. Le projet s'est développé dans deux écoles d'enseignement primaire de la ville de Jaca, au nord de la province de Huesca, en Espagne, qui se trouve à 20 kilomètres de la frontière française. La proximité du pays voisin met les élèves en situation d'un besoin réel d'apprentissage du français. De même, la région d'Oloron Sainte Marie et la vallée d'Aspe en France retrouvent la même situation dans leurs écoles avec l'apprentissage de l'espagnol.

Le but était de créer la possibilité pour les élèves espagnols de communiquer dans la langue cible, le français, avec des élèves français qui ont fait de même en espagnol. Cette communication a eu lieu pendant une année scolaire, au moyen de la correspondance écrite, avec comme finalité une rencontre avec les correspondants français à la fin de l'année.

2.   Contexte local

La ville de Jaca est située au nord de la région de l'Aragon en Espagne, dans la province de Huesca, à 20 kilomètres de la frontière française. Les Pyrénées ont toujours été une barrière naturelle, mais, malgré tout, il y a toujours eu une grande tradition de relation avec la région voisine. On peut parler des relations commerciales et personnelles; cependant, il ne faut pas oublier la vague d'émigrants espagnols dans le sud de la France à cause de la guerre civile espagnole.

Avec la construction du tunnel du Somport, les deux pays se sont rapprochés. La région de Jaca est une région très touristique, avec un grand développement du tourisme de montagne et sports d'hiver et avec un échange commercial important avec la région d'Aquitaine en France. La proximité d'une grande ville française comme Pau fait que les Espagnols profitent des jours fériés pour y aller faire du tourisme, pour faire des échanges sportifs et pour y aller faire des courses. Jaca est une ville d'environ 11 000 habitants qui vit, principalement, du tourisme et des services. Il faut noter, aussi, une population militaire importante et d'autres secteurs qui travaillent dans l'agriculture et l'élevage. Pendant les périodes de vacances, la population augmente considérablement. Il y a un climat de montagne, avec des hivers longs et froids et des printemps pluvieux.

L'école Monte Oroel se situe dans le nord de la ville, à côté de la gare de trains et proche du mont Rapitán. Il fait partie du Quartier Nord qui se caractérise par des maisons hétérogènes. La population est originaire de la ville et des alentours. Il y a un pourcentage important d'immigrants qui, dans la plupart des cas, reste stable. A 100 mètres à peu près se trouve le Lycée Pirineos, auquel le centre est adscrit. Dans cette zone, on trouve le quartier San Jorge, dont les habitants sont d'ethnie gitane. Les enfants de ce quartier vont aussi à l'école Monte Oroel. La plupart des élèves habitent près de l'école et peuvent venir à pied ou en bus urbain. L'école S. Juan de la Peña se situe au sud de la ville. Cette école dispose de services de ramassage scolaire pour les élèves qui vivent dans les villages de la région.

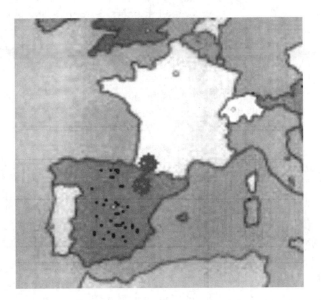

3.   Buts et objectifs

a)   Motiver les élèves à l'apprentissage d'une langue étrangère.

b)   Apprendre à communiquer avec des personnes d'un autre pays avec une langue et une culture différentes.

c)   Découvrir une culture, des coutumes et des loisirs différents.

d)   Augmenter les connaissances linguistiques et culturelles des apprenants dans un environnement authentique.

e)   Découvrir de nouveaux endroits et personnes.

f)   Développer l'expression orale et écrite dans un contexte réel.

g)   Développer des attitudes d'ouverture et de tolérance.

h)   Mettre en valeur et en pratique le sens d'une Europe sans frontières.

4. Public cible

Cette activité a été conçue pour les élèves apprenants de français dans les écoles primaires publiques Monte Oroel et San Juan de la Peña de Jaca (Huesca) en Espagne. En Espagne, l'apprentissage d'une langue étrangère est obligatoire dès l'âge de 8 ans, trois heures par semaine, depuis la Loi de Réforme de l'Education en 1992. Dans la plupart des écoles, la langue étudiée est l'anglais, mais dans ces deux écoles, les élèves ont le choix entre l'anglais et le français, étant donné que les parents sont très conscients de l'utilité de la langue française dans cette région. A l'école Monte Oroel, il y a une trentaine d'élèves qui étudient le français et à l'école S. Juan de la Peña, il y en a à peu près 65. Cela donne, en tout, une centaine d'élèves.

5. Organisation de la correspondance

Etant donné que la correspondance a eu lieu dans deux écoles différentes, l'organisation a été, elle-même, différente en fonction des disponibilités et des projets qui ont été conçus avec les collègues français, même si l'enseignante était la même personne qui se déplaçait dans les deux écoles.

Pour l'école Monte Oroel, ce sont les enfants espagnols qui ont écrit la première lettre et les enfants français ont choisi un correspondant en fonction de leurs goûts et préférences. Ils n'ont pas tenu compte de l'âge et du sexe du correspondant. Pour l'école S. Juan de la Peña, nous avons orienté la correspondance de façon à ce que les enfants soient du même âge et du même sexe. Les filles avaient des correspondantes filles et les garçons des garçons. Certaines filles ont eu deux correspondantes en raison du nombre élevé d'enfants.

Nous avons observé qu'à cet âge, les garçons préfèrent écrire à des garçons et les filles à des filles; cependant, dans les deux écoles, le système a fonctionné et les enfants se sont vite habitués aux correspondants qu'ils ont eus. Dans les écoles, il y a quatre niveaux de français. Pour les apprenants qui venaient juste de commencer, un modèle de lettre a été écrit au tableau qu'ils ont pu modifier ou changer. Les premières lettres étaient des lettres de présentation: je m'appelle … j'habite à … j'ai … ans, etc.… Après, ils ont décoré les lettres avec des dessins. Les autres groupes pouvaient les écrire tous seuls, mais on pouvait écrire au tableau des mots ou expressions (annexe 1).

Tout au long de l'année, les enfants ont pu mettre en pratique ce qu'ils ont appris en cours. Par exemple, quand ils ont appris le vocabulaire lié à la maison, ils ont décrit leur propre maison, quand ils ont travaillé sur la description physique, ils se sont décrits, quand ils ont traité de la nourriture, ils ont raconté ce qu'ils mangent au petit-déjeuner ou au goûter, les animaux et les couleurs pour exprimer leurs goûts. Nous en avons également profité aussi pour leur faire découvrir la civilisation espagnole et française: les jours fériés, comment on fête le carnaval, Noël, Pâques, etc.

Les enfants ont également préparé de petits cadeaux qu'ils ont envoyés, des dessins, des photos, des autocollants et des cartes postales. La correspondance a favorisé l'échange de productions des élèves: des lettres personnelles, un journal de classe, des articles de journaux, des photos, etc. Au niveau de la correction, on a essayé de laisser les lettres telles que les apprenants les ont écrites, sauf si les fautes empêchaient de comprendre le sens de la lettre. On voulait que ça soit naturel et ne pas corriger automatiquement toutes les erreurs.

6.   Organisation des échanges

Suite à la correspondance établie pendant l'année scolaire, nous avons organisé les échanges de manière différente pour les deux écoles espagnoles.

Ecole Monte Oroel

Dans cette école, l'échange a eu lieu a la fin de l'année scolaire, au mois de juin, avec la totalité des élèves qui étudiaient le français, c'est-à-dire quatre niveaux différents, soit une totalité d'une trentaine d'enfants. Nous avons fixé deux dates avec les enseignants français de l'école de Bedous, dans la vallée d'Aspe. Nous avons eu une réunion préalable, à l'école de Bedous, pour la mise au point des rencontres. Nous avons décidé de faire la rencontre sur deux jours. Le premier jour, un vendredi, les élèves espagnols se sont déplacés à Bedous et le deuxième jour, deux semaines plus tard, les enfants français sont venus nous rendre visite à Jaca.

La région de Jaca, bien qu'elle se trouve en montagne, est très touristique et plus urbaine que la région de nos correspondants ; c'est la raison par laquelle nous avons décidé, avec nos collègues français, d'organiser à Bedous une visite du milieu rural, du village et de leur entourage. Nous avons visité une exploitation laitière, une coopérative fromagère et nous avons fait une randonnée à la campagne et un pique-nique en plein air.

Cependant, avant de commencer les visites, nous avons organisé un jeu de présentation pour que les enfants se reconnaissent. En effet, il y avait eu une correspondance pendant toute l'année scolaire, mais ils ne s'étaient jamais rencontrés. Le jeu consistait à reconnaître leur correspondant par moyen des animaux. Les enfants espagnols avaient accroché à leurs vêtements le dessin d'un animal que les enfants français avaient envoyé et ils devaient imiter le cri de cet animal.

Deux semaines plus tard, un vendredi aussi, nous avons reçu nos correspondants français à Jaca. La visite, ici, s'est organisée dans le sens contraire. Puisque les enfants français venaient d'un milieu rural, nous avons organisé une journée plus touristique et urbaine. Nous avons visité la Mairie et nous avons été reçus par le Maire qui leur a souhaité la bienvenue, avec quelques minutes de questions et réponses. Ensuite, nous sommes allés visiter la citadelle du XVIIème siècle et nous sommes allés à la patinoire municipale. Le pique-nique a eu lieu dans un parc de la ville. Nous avons fait une petite promenade en ville avant de faire les adieux à nos correspondants.

Ecole San Juan de la Peña

A l'école S. Juan de la Peña, nous avons fait un projet différent avec nos collègues français. Nous avons eu une réunion préalable dans une auberge de montagne en France, à mi-chemin entre Jaca et les villages français qui allaient participer à cet échange, pour mettre au point le projet.

Nous avons décidé de faire une seule rencontre sur deux jours au mois de juin pour rester dormir à l'auberge que nous avons visitée à l'occasion de cette réunion. Etant donné que l'école S. Juan de la Peña est très grande, le groupe d'élèves de français est très nombreux. Nous avons organisé l'échange pour les trois premiers niveaux, puisque le dernier niveau fait un voyage de fin d'année avec l'école. Malgré cela, le groupe était encore très nombreux et l'auberge n'avait pas assez de place, ce qui nous a obligé à faire deux groupes. Les deux premières années d'élèves de français viendraient un mardi et mercredi, tandis que la troisième année viendrait le mardi et le mercredi de la semaine d'après.

Les deux premières années ont établi la correspondance avec trois petites écoles françaises: Bidos, Eysus et une école d'Oloron Sainte Marie et les autres avec deux autres écoles: Verdets et Estialesq. L'organisation de deux rencontres s'est déroulée de la même façon. Le premier jour, les enfants espagnols sont allés passer la journée dans les écoles de leurs correspondants. Il a fallu prévoir des collègues pour accompagner les enfants, au moins un instituteur espagnol par école. Dans les écoles françaises, nos collègues avaient préparé des activités: des jeux, des danses régionales, des lotos, du ping-pong … et les repas à la cantine de l'école. A la fin de la journée scolaire, le car est venu nous chercher pour aller vers l'auberge de montagne, qui est sur la route de retour de l'Espagne. Nous nous sommes arrêtés pour visiter la Maison du Parc National des Pyrénées à Etsaut, expliqué par un guide du Parc.

Vers 18 heures 30, nous sommes arrivés à l'auberge, nous avons distribué les chambres avec l'aide du personnel de l'auberge et nous avons dîné à 19 heures. Ensuite, les enfants on fait des jeux et sont allés se coucher. Le lendemain, nous avons fait une randonnée en montagne avec deux guides spécialisés sur le circuit de ski de fond, nous avons pique-niqué en montagne et, à la fin de la journée, nous sommes repartis (annexe 2).

Il faut dire que la mise en situation a été totale. Les enfants espagnols on pu découvrir une autre culture et façon de vivre si différente, bien que nous soyons à une heure de route seulement. Les enfants espagnols ont par exemple été très choqués par les horaires. En Espagne, on mange à 13 heures 30 et en France à 12 heures 30. De même, nous avons l'habitude de dîner vers 21 heures et en France à 19 heures.

7.   Financement des échanges

Les échanges ont été financés selon les pourcentages suivants:

- 50%: subvention économique des régions de l'Aragon et de l'Aquitaine pour des projets éducatifs;
- 30%: les parents d'élèves;
- 20%: l'école.

Lors des visites dans la ville de Jaca, les entrées de la patinoire et les entrées de la Citadelle ont été financées par la Mairie de la ville.

8.   Difficultés rencontrées

Pour pouvoir mener à terme la correspondance et les échanges, nous avons rencontré plusieurs difficultés, telles que:

- trouver des écoles motivées par le projet;
- trouver des enseignants qui s'engagent à faire suivre la correspondance et à mettre en place les rencontres;
- groupes d'enfants assez nombreux en Espagne par rapport aux écoles françaises;
- prévoir d'autres collègues comme accompagnateurs;
- en France, l'apprentissage d'une langue étrangère à l'école primaire n'est pas obligatoire;
- assurer la continuité des échanges.

9.   Résultats

Pour avoir un aperçu des résultats atteints avec la correspondance et les échanges, nous avons préparé un petit questionnaire que tous les enfants espagnols participants aux échanges ont rempli (annexe 3). Nous pouvons observer les réponses aux six questions et les trois réponses pour lesquelles ils avaient le choix entre: très intéressant, assez intéressant et peu intéressant. Le questionnaire a été rempli par 70 élèves. Vous pouvez lire dans l'annexe 3 les questions qui correspondent à chaque numéro de 1 à 6.

Nous nous apercevons que les réponses les plus positives pour les enfants correspondent aux questions 4, 5 et 6. Cinquante et un enfants sur soixante-dix pensent qu'il est très intéressant d'aller en France pour pratiquer la langue. Quarante-quatre enfants sur soixante-dix croient qu'il est très important d'avoir des correspondants pour pratiquer la langue. Et quarante-six enfants sur soixante-dix sont plus motivés pour apprendre la langue grâce à la proximité et l'utilité de la langue. La réponse la moins positive a été la question numéro trois, étant donné que 8 enfants sur 70 ont dit qu'ils n'ont pas pu mettre en pratique ce qu'ils ont appris en cours de français. Par rapport aux trois premières questions, les réponses étaient presque au même niveau concernant « très intéressant » et « assez intéressant ».

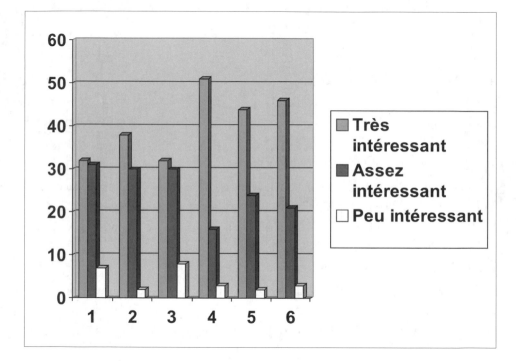

10. Attentes en ce qui concerne le projet

A la question sur leurs attentes en ce qui concerne l'échange et la correspondance, les élèves avaient le choix de répondre par écrit ou en faisant un dessin (annexe 4). Vous pouvez lire ci-dessous les attentes des enfants:

- « J'aimerai me faire de nouveaux amis »;

- « Faire des activités avec nos correspondants »;

- « Je veux dormir dans une grande chambre avec mes amis »;

- « Pouvoir jouer avec les correspondants français »;

- « Pratiquer la langue française »;

- « Je voudrais visiter Paris, apprendre à parler en français et manger de la nourriture française »;

- « Visiter de nouveaux villages, faire des amis, connaître leurs coutumes »;

- « Je voudrais leur faire visiter notre école »;

- « Je voudrais connaître sa famille »;

- « Aller à la patinoire »;

- « Que mon correspondant ait les mêmes goûts que moi »;

- « J'aimerai connaître des enfants d'autres pays »;

- « Je voudrais aller chez mon correspondant et faire beaucoup de crêpes »;

- « Je voudrais visiter la Tour Eiffel et monter le plus haut possible »;

- « J'espère recevoir de belles lettres »;

- « Que les correspondants français pratiquent l'espagnol »;

- « Aller à la plage à Bayonne »;

- « Jouer au foot avec nos correspondants »;

- « Que l'auberge ait un terrain de foot et une piscine et qu'elle se trouve à la montagne ».

11. Conclusion

En conclusion, nous pouvons affirmer que l'échange scolaire a été un bon moyen pour motiver les élèves à l'apprentissage d'une langue étrangère et a joué un rôle très important pour la pratique de la langue. Les élèves ont pu utiliser la langue dans un environnement authentique. Cela a également été une bonne occasion pour découvrir un autre pays, une autre culture et des coutumes différentes. La tolérance et le respect sont en effet très importantes pour l'ouverture de l'Europe et pour les relations interculturelles. Il faut souligner les bonnes relations qui se sont établies entre les élèves et leur souhait de continuer les échanges les années à venir. Les enfants se sont montrés très enthousiastes et motivés et cette activité a permis de vivre des expériences personnelles très enrichissantes dans le cadre d'une activité scolaire atteignant de cette façon les objectifs proposés. L'expérience a été très positive et il serait très intéressant de pouvoir continuer dans l'avenir.

12. Remerciements

Je remercie mes élèves, mes collègues des écoles Monte Oroel et San Juan de la Peña de Jaca (Huesca), Espagne, et les élèves et collègues français qui ont participé à ce projet.

Bonjour l damien

Ça va?

J m' apelle Gabriel et toi?

J'ai 9 ans et toi?

J'aime patije fot-dall et esport d'hiver et toi?

Mon ecole 'apelle San Juan de la paria

J'ai des poisons

A U revoir

Salut!

Je m'appelle Maryïa. Et toi?

J'ai 9 ans. Et toi?

J'aime le patinage sur glace.

Mon école s'appelle San Juan de la Peña.

J'aime les chevaux.

À bientôt

Maryïa

Annexe 2

Annexe 3

1. Comment as-tu trouvé la correspondance avec les élèves français?

- o   Très intéressante
- o   Assez intéressante
- o   Peu intéressante

2. Comment as-tu trouvé l'échange avec les élèves français?

- o   Très intéressant
- o   Assez intéressant
- o   Peu intéressant

3. As-tu pu mettre en pratique avec les élèves français ce que tu as appris en cours de français?

- o   Oui
- o   Quelques fois
- o   Non

4. Penses-tu qu'il est important d'aller en France pour pratiquer la langue?

- o   Très important
- o   Assez important
- o   Peu important

5. Penses-tu qu'il est important d'avoir des correspondants français pour pratiquer la langue?

- o   Très important
- o   Assez important
- o   Peu important

6. Te sens-tu plus motivé(e) pour apprendre le français parce que tu vois que c'est une langue utile pour toi et, en plus, que nous habitons à 20 km. de la France?

- o   Très motivé(e)
- o   Assez motivé(e)
- o   Peu motivé(e)

Annexe 4

149

Agents de vente des publications du Conseil de l'Europe
Sales agents for publications of the Council of Europe

BELGIUM/BELGIQUE
La Librairie européenne SA
50, avenue A. Jonnart
B-1200 BRUXELLES 20
Tel.: (32) 2 734 0281
Fax: (32) 2 735 0860
E-mail: info@libeurop.be
http://www.libeurop.be

Jean de Lannoy
202, avenue du Roi
B-1190 BRUXELLES
Tel.: (32) 2 538 4308
Fax: (32) 2 538 0841
E-mail: jean.de.lannoy@euronet.be
http://www.jean-de-lannoy.be

CANADA
Renouf Publishing Company Limited
5369 Chemin Canotek Road
CDN-OTTAWA, Ontario, K1J 9J3
Tel.: (1) 613 745 2665
Fax: (1) 613 745 7660
E-mail: order.dept@renoufbooks.com
http://www.renoufbooks.com

CZECH REPUBLIC/RÉP. TCHÈQUE
Suweco Cz Dovoz Tisku Praha
Ceskomoravska 21
CZ-18021 PRAHA 9
Tel.: (420) 2 660 35 364
Fax: (420) 2 683 30 42
E-mail: import@suweco.cz

DENMARK/DANEMARK
GAD Direct
Fiolstaede 31-33
DK-1171 KOBENHAVN K
Tel.: (45) 33 13 72 33
Fax: (45) 33 12 54 94
E-mail: info@gaddirect.dk

FINLAND/FINLANDE
Akateeminen Kirjakauppa
Keskuskatu 1, PO Box 218
FIN-00381 HELSINKI
Tel.: (358) 9 121 41
Fax: (358) 9 121 4450
E-mail: akatilaus@stockmann.fi
http://www.akatilaus.akateeminen.com

GERMANY/ALLEMAGNE
AUSTRIA/AUTRICHE
UNO Verlag
August Bebel Allee 6
D-53175 BONN
Tel.: (49) 2 28 94 90 20
Fax: (49) 2 28 94 90 222
E-mail: bestellung@uno-verlag.de
http://www.uno-verlag.de

GREECE/GRÈCE
Librairie Kauffmann
Mavrokordatou 9
GR-ATHINAI 106 78
Tel.: (30) 1 38 29 283
Fax: (30) 1 38 33 967
E-mail: ord@otenet.gr

HUNGARY/HONGRIE
Euro Info Service
Hungexpo Europa Kozpont ter 1
H-1101 BUDAPEST
Tel.: (361) 264 8270
Fax: (361) 264 8271
E-mail: euroinfo@euroinfo.hu
http://www.euroinfo.hu

ITALY/ITALIE
Libreria Commissionaria Sansoni
Via Duca di Calabria 1/1, CP 552
I-50125 FIRENZE
Tel.: (39) 556 4831
Fax: (39) 556 41257
E-mail: licosa@licosa.com
http://www.licosa.com

NETHERLANDS/PAYS-BAS
De Lindeboom Internationale Publikaties
PO Box 202, MA de Ruyterstraat 20 A
NL-7480 AE HAAKSBERGEN
Tel.: (31) 53 574 0004
Fax: (31) 53 572 9296
E-mail: lindeboo@worldonline.nl
http://home-1-orldonline.nl/~lindeboo/

NORWAY/NORVÈGE
Akademika, A/S Universitetsbokhandel
PO Box 84, Blindern
N-0314 OSLO
Tel.: (47) 22 85 30 30
Fax: (47) 23 12 24 20

POLAND/POLOGNE
Głowna Księgarnia Naukowa
im. B. Prusa
Krakowskie Przedmiescie 7
PL-00-068 WARSZAWA
Tel.: (48) 29 22 66
Fax: (48) 22 26 64 49
E-mail: inter@internews.com.pl
http://www.internews.com.pl

PORTUGAL
Livraria Portugal
Rua do Carmo, 70
P-1200 LISBOA
Tel.: (351) 13 47 49 82
Fax: (351) 13 47 02 64
E-mail: liv.portugal@mail.telepac.pt

SPAIN/ESPAGNE
Mundi-Prensa Libros SA
Castelló 37
E-28001 MADRID
Tel.: (34) 914 36 37 00
Fax: (34) 915 75 39 98
E-mail: libreria@mundiprensa.es
http://www.mundiprensa.com

SWITZERLAND/SUISSE
Adeco – Van Diermen
Chemin du Lacuez 41
CH-1807 BLONAY
Tel.: (41) 21 943 26 73
Fax: (41) 21 943 36 05
E-mail: info@adeco.org

UNITED KINGDOM/ROYAUME-UNI
TSO (formerly HMSO)
51 Nine Elms Lane
GB-LONDON SW8 5DR
Tel.: (44) 207 873 8372
Fax: (44) 207 873 8200
E-mail: customer.services@theso.co.uk
http://www.the-stationery-office.co.uk
http://www.itsofficial.net

UNITED STATES and CANADA/
ÉTATS-UNIS et CANADA
Manhattan Publishing Company
468 Albany Post Road, PO Box 850
CROTON-ON-HUDSON,
NY 10520, USA
Tel.: (1) 914 271 5194
Fax: (1) 914 271 5856
E-mail: Info@manhattanpublishing.com
http://www.manhattanpublishing.com

FRANCE
La Documentation française
(Diffusion/Vente France entière)
124 rue H. Barbusse
93308 Aubervilliers Cedex
Tel.: (33) 01 40 15 70 00
Fax: (33) 01 40 15 68 00
E-mail: vel@ladocfrancaise.gouv.fr
http://www.ladocfrancaise.gouv.fr

Librairie Kléber (Vente Strasbourg)
Palais de l'Europe
F-67075 Strasbourg Cedex
Fax: (33) 03 88 52 91 21
E-mail: librairie.kleber@coe.int

Council of Europe Publishing/Editions du Conseil de l'Europe
F-67075 Strasbourg Cedex
Tel.: (33) 03 88 41 25 81 – Fax: (33) 03 88 41 39 10 – E-mail: publishing@coe.int – Website: http://book.coe.int